Rogue Ministry

The REAL story of the authentic, unorthodox international mission of Fred Kornis, Jr.

by Fred Kornis, Jr.

with Anthony Merizzi

Publishing support, design, and composition by 4PlayBooks.com

ISBN-13: 978-1985201439   ISBN-10: 1985201437

Printed in the United States of America
R 3.21.18.1

All proceeds from the sale of this book will go to the mission outreach of Heartland International Ministries, Inc.

DEDICATION

To our family. My amazing wife has stood faithfully by my side for over 50 years now. There are no words to do justice to her longsuffering love (1 Corinthians 13) and grace during all the years of my out of control anger, lust and intensity. It would have destroyed us and our family, but Barb overcame my abuse with the love and supernatural reality of Jesus! Thank you Barb! XOXO

Barb has helped raise our four wonderful children: Summer, Jeremy, Faith and Vanessa, who have turned into amazing adults. From these four kids, have come 15 amazing grandchildren: Autumn, Rebecca, Zachary, Kelsey, Evan, Gabrielle, Emmalee, Noah, Quentin, Spencer, Toby, Ava, Calvin, Rosie, and Penelope; and two great-grandchildren: Macy and Maverick!!

We are a wonderful, nearly perfect, normal, dysfunctional family!! This book is dedicated to our family's past and future generations! Praise the Lord!

"You will never make a good impression on other people until you stop thinking about what sort of impression you are making. Even in literature and art, no man who bothers about originality will ever be original: whereas if you simply try to tell the truth (without caring two pence how often it has been told before) you will, nine times out of ten, become original without ever having noticed it... Give up yourself, and you will find your real self."

-- *C.S. Lewis, Mere Christianity*

"And you will seek Me and find Me, when you search for Me with all your heart."

-- *Jeremiah 29:13*

CONTENTS

ROGUE MINISTRY

ACKNOWLEDGMENTS

It is impossible to express the proper thanks and appreciation to all the people who have encouraged and influenced my life. I will spend part of eternity trying to do justice in acknowledging and thanking so many people. I take that future reunion very seriously.

Thank you to George Verwer, founder of Operation Mobilization, who has been my earthly hero and mentor since the night in 1972 in St. Petersburg, Florida, when I woke him up at 4 AM. I had been unable to sleep after hearing his heart and vision about the world. I knew if what he'd said about unreached people was true... I could never, ever be a normal person again. Through the years he has called, visited, provided literature and kept me sober about the dangers that could ruin a life and ministry. His classic book Messiology gives me hope -- because I am so messy!!

Thank you to Vicky Rogers, a true "southern belle," uprooted her life and moved to Kansas City to provide the basic administration and office support that freed me up to GO for so many years. Her book, A Life Not My Own, is a testament to her selfless service, to me personally and to the kingdom of God. As a single woman, she gave her life, tremendous skills and absolute integrity, to protect this rogue minister.

Since Vicky was so irreplaceable, God had to send us an "angel" to replace her when she retired. Angel and Travis Hecht, along with their three children, Tanner, Spencer, and Lexi, are from Wamego, KS, "The Land of Oz." For almost five years, she has taken on many impossible tasks for HIM, all while battling some health issues and dealing with endless administration, financial, and staff issues. She has also ministered in India, the Philippines, Nicaragua, and the USA as a missionary herself. Somewhere in the middle of all of that, she has professionally typed, edited and organized 40 years' worth of my diaries, journals, and history… and she's been a big part in making this book possible. Incredible! Muchas gracias, Angel!

Thank you to each of our PALS (Partner and Leader Servants) of Heartland International Ministries, who have allowed me to be part of their families and ministries in the most unbelievable places. Together we have seen multitudes "enlightened" with the inner reality of the living God.

Thank you to the beloved Canaanite woman who boldly confronted the very God of creation with an almost rebuking statement, saying, "Even the dogs get the crumbs from under the table" (Matthew 15:21-28). Wow!? I can't wait to meet her. Women like her, who know how to converse with God so intimately and practically, have helped me to deliver more "crumbs" throughout my life.

To Byron Whetstone, Angel Hecht, Tom Blasco, Cheryl Popek-Rice, and all the other past and future HIM Board Members who have and continue to provide such vital support and leadership to our mission and to me personally. THANK YOU and God bless you!!

Thanks to Anthony Merizzi, my incredible writing coach and partner in this project, who has helped make this book possible with his wise, creative, and patient style.

To Honey, our adorable, "sweet and sticky" puppy, who has more sensitivity, loyalty, sympathy, and unconditional love than any human I've ever met! I'm sure God will have a place for dear creatures like her in heaven!

Lastly, and most importantly, Barb, I don't know where I'd be had you not come into my life. God will perfectly reward you in heaven forever for always supporting me. Your unique prayer life and relationship with the Lord is as "rogue" as it gets. Sorry about trading your car for a motorcycle.

ROGUE MINISTRY

FOREWORD

It has been a joy to follow and share in your unique ministry for the past 30 years. As I reflect on what you have done, the first thought that comes to me is that it is distinctly modern, in that yours is a ministry that could not have been done before you did it. Only the last half of the twentieth century has offered the opportunity to travel widely with as many resources. You have, no doubt, logged more miles for the cause of Christ than all the pioneer missionaries combined in the first 25 years of modern missions!

Your ministry is clearly unique because few venture into so many diverse cultures, for few can stand the stresses of it. Yet, you have done so, with a sensitive and understanding heart, strengthening and training the brethren in one place, evangelizing in another, organizing relief here, planting a church there. I suppose what I am most thankful for is that you have not done it with ease or have just taken it in stride. Yes, few can stand the stresses of what you do, and are either unable or unwilling to do it. But you are willing and further, you are obedient despite the cost.

I have seen that cost. I have seen it in the agony of spirit as the weight of the care of so many presses in on your soul. I have seen it in the godly jealousy over the huge gap that exists between the tremendous resources of a largely apathetic American church, and the zeal of those dear ones who have so little in other parts of the world yet have such an enormous task ahead of them. I have seen it in your quest for balance when there was so much to keep you off balance. Thank God that I can't call you a "consummate professional!" Passion, compassion, zeal and tears were all the hallmarks of the blood-soaked ministry of our Lord Jesus. "It is the way the Master went, should not the servant tread it still." You have. PRAISE THE LORD!

Another gospel song says, "Ready to go, ready to stay, ready my place to fill." I think of that song when I remember that, while your heart beats for worldwide evangelism and discipleship, yet God has also called you to a ministry at home of revival and encouragement for the American church. You have based your personal ministry in a local church and have even been willing to be a part of that structure from time to time when called upon. This also is rare among the independent-spirited missionary evangelists. The fact that you choose to be a part of our church throughout my 13 years as pastor remains something that I treasure as one of the most significant encouragements and affirmations of my ministry.

You have been enabled to be "ready to go or stay" because of the best that God has given you for ministry - Barbara. Most people who do the world hopping you do, do it "by faith." You have seen the provision of God, but it has taken wise management. You, and your children, have all been in this together. Many have seen the sacrifices and struggles, but also the sweetness of the awareness that you are in the center of God's will.

Thank you, Fred and Barb! You said, "Yes" to one another, and both of you said "yes" to the Lord. And thank you, Lord, for the profound work of grace that has given these precious ones to the church worldwide for the salvation and encouragement of many souls.

Sincerely in Christ,
Pastor David and Mary Brown
Former Senior Pastor-
First Baptist Church, Shawnee, KS.

> "You snakes!! You poisonous snakes!! How can
> you escape being condemned to hell?"
>
> *Jesus, Matthew 23:33*

CHAPTER 1
"YOU GOIN' TO HEAVEN OR HELL, KORNIS?"

The young soldier was already a ticking time bomb, looking for a place to explode. He didn't need some old woman chewing him out over a simple request. Not today.

Standing in the sun-baked Lawson Field hangar at Fort Benning, Georgia, he'd just dropped a bundle of used parachutes on the floor. Some of the chutes were simply in need of a quick seam repair, their canopies largely intact but a little rough around the edges. Others were a worn-out bundle of silk threads and faded netting that had been torn and patched so often, they made a Raggedy Andy doll look like a GQ model.

Remarkably, most of the parachutes still hadn't disintegrated completely from the years of abuse they'd known. With a little patchwork and a little faith, the chutes could be restored back into service again, and probably survive a few more ripcord pulls out the side of a C130's jump door.

That's why the young soldier was at the hangar again today, to get the old-lady seamstress to work her magic on each chute's silk once again. He had no intention of listening to another Bible-thumping lecture by the crazy old gal, though.

"You got to git born agin!" she proclaimed in her ancient Southern twang, pulling a crumpled parachute onto the table as she sat cross-legged in a folding chair. "Yer life's in a tumble, boy. What you gonna do about it?"

The paratrooper rolled his eyes and gritted his teeth, holding back the raging fury that was always boiling just below the surface. After working his way up to platoon leader on the team, he had finally found a job he was good at, probably for the first time in his life. He'd gotten used to swallowing his fears so often that they'd barely even registered as a blink in his eye anymore. Adn he'd proven he was tough enough... time and time again.

No flinch, no hesitation. Even when the troop's Commanding Officer would grab a freshly-patched parachute from the pile and throw it to him from across the hangar.

" Jump it," the CO would bark.

"Yes, sir!" the boy snapped back with a salute.

"Don't sass me with words, soldier," the officer would shout. "Get this parachute strapped to your back, and get your ass on the next plane goin' up across that runway. If the chute holds when you jump, we'll know soon enough if Esther's sewing and your packing did the job."

That's how life worked for the paratrooper now, and he loved the adventure and rough-and-tumble unpredictability of it all. Still, there was a semblance of order to most days - even a few clear expectations to go along with the drills, discipline and demands of his military life.

Expectations... now there's a word he'd never learned to abide by. Ever since he'd popped into the world of his young teenaged parents in the 1950s, he hadn't been held back by expectations for more than a single minute at a time. Instead, he'd grown up in Kansas City, Missouri with a gut-feeling of spontaneity and full-throttle commitment relentlessly driving him.

As a toddler and the oldest of three boys, he sensed the extreme contrast between his mother and father's personal approaches. He felt his father's explosive, rough-around-the-edges physical presence in the home, and his mother's sensitive, almost artistic personality. Looking through a preschooler's eyes, he couldn't see the early signs of their marriage coming apart.

Yet he'd always remembered his father's old-fashioned reverence for creation, and how the man would sometimes take his boys out to the backyard at night, where they'd all lay on their backs looking up at the sky. As a young child, he became fascinated with the stars, moon, and the great universe around them. All through those years, star-gazing with his dad planted a hunger to know about the wonder of the galaxies.

The boy was in kindergarten or first grade when his father moved the family to California, to work with a friend who'd offered him a job. When his dad soon found out that something was going on between that friend and his own young wife, the man went absolutely ballistic.

In fact, that endured as one of the paratrooper's earliest childhood memories. The night he watched as his ex-boxer father picked up every piece of furniture in their little apartment and smashed it to pieces will be forever etched in his mind and heart. After destroying the place like a bear in a china closet, he loaded the boys into his car in the middle of the night, and drove all the way from California to Kansas City without stopping.

Back then, his father's righteous indignation and jealousy were so fiery and dangerous. The trauma of his outburst was like the seed of life for the young boy. From that point on, he was just surviving.

Not long after that initial explosion, his mother came back to his father's house. The young couple tried to make it work as a family again, living in a country home on three acres of land in the rural town of Stanley, Kansas. They raised their own chickens, fresh eggs, and milk, and even built a raft for the boys to float down the creek on sun-drenched summer days. In truth, their family lived on eggshells for another two or three years.

There really wasn't ever the time for any kind of "churchy" stuff. The boys never saw the inside of a church or Sunday school, let alone Bible camps or anything like that. In fact, as time went on, the oldest boy grew into a confirmed skeptic, hiding in the woods beside a nearby Nazarene Bible camp and thinking those Bible-thumpers were all crazy.

Unfortunately, through all this time, the "other man" was still courting his mother with love letters. When the letters were discovered, his mother finally left for good. She simply called a taxi, and told her oldest son Freddie that she was going to a nearby town to rest for a couple of days.

There was no way the boy could know that, as she stepped off the sidewalk beside a tiny sapling he had planted in the front yard, she was going to California... and she was never coming back.

When his father returned from work later that night, he knew instantly that something was wrong. "Why did you let her go?!" he raged, shaking the shocked youngster to traumatized tears.

Within weeks, the house was sold. While his father battled to get legal custody of his three sons, he passed the boys off to friends and relatives for almost a year, until he could get his life organized again as a single parent. Aunts, uncles, and friends took the boys in to help his dad survive. Everyone pulling together was wonderful, but there was a lot to that time that he'd never know about.

Eventually, the boy's dad found another place to live in the suburbs of Kansas City, in a town called Roeland Park. From then on, they all lived in a guy's world.

There was never a woman in his father's house for the rest of his childhood. Between his dad and his two brothers, Buddy and Benny, the four guys did all the housework, cooking, and laundry. They also took care of whatever schedule-keeping, parenting and extra-curricular activities that needed to be done. On Sundays, his father made up enough foil-wrapped TV dinners to last all week. He always made sure the boys would always have enough to eat while he was away at work.

Trouble was, with his dad putting in 12-hour days, there was a lot of family turmoil -- and very little guidance or supervision. It didn't take long for the oldest boy to become a full-blown juvenile delinquent. His dad couldn't keep up with him by the time he was hitting junior high school.

Even as a young adolescent living in a world he couldn't comprehend, the oldest boy realized how destructive he could be. He was petrified, because deep down he knew it was getting serious… and dangerous.

With each day tumbling into the next, he was constantly getting involved in a lot of petty crimes. One day, sitting in his fourth or fifth grade classroom in a little school called East Antioch, he was shocked as everyone in the class looked out the window to watch a uniformed policeman approaching the door.

They were coming for him!

"Jump it", the CO barked

Of course, the boy knew he had vandalized somebody's house the day before, breaking into the basement with another buddy (his best friend Steve, who later was to become an infamous bank robber) and covering the walls with spray paint and some caulking guns. When the cops sat him down in the principal's office and asked him why he did it, he told them it was just a crazy time being wild, and it was just for excitement. His father would have to pay big bucks for this vandalism spree; the first of many

21

more to come.

That was officially the beginning of his criminal life. He became a wild thing, with plenty of vandalism and run-ins with the law to follow.

By the time the young man made it to high school in the mid-60s, he'd found drugs and rock and roll, playing in bands and becoming notorious as a wild dancer and a music entertainer at the same time. Many of his fans called him the best dancer in Kansas City, and everybody stood back when he put on a show. They were in awe of his signature move, jumping off the stage and landing in the splits on the floor among the party-goers.

As a teenager, he seemed to feed on making a spectacle. He was usually out of control, doing anything that brought a thrill. Yet through it all, he was walking a tightrope with his father, a former Golden Gloves boxer with a quick temper. On days when his trousers hid the welts on the back of his thighs from the belt-whipping he'd received the night before, the boy would boil in quiet fury... seasoned with shame as he realized that his father's rage was mixed with brokenness, sometimes even in tears over the boy's reckless actions.

It was breaking his father's heart.

Still, as he approached his high-school graduation year, the boy's deep-seated anger increased his defiance. He harvested some marijuana in Lawrence, Kansas, and took an extended trip to California to sell pot, buying LSD and other hard-core drugs to try while he was there. The pace of his adventures continued to race by, sometimes even faster than life itself.

Against all odds, he finally graduated from high school in 1968 alongside Phil McGraw, one of his fellow students who would become famous as television's Dr. Phil in later years. Back then, within months of graduation, the boy began a sexual relationship with one of his high-school teachers, and continued his impulsive, drug-fueled path through life.

On a trip to Arizona that same year, he arrived at his former teacher's home so stoned that she frantically sobered him up and took him to the Army recruiter in town. The woman recognized how horribly close he was to putting his own life in danger, and she probably saved his life at that point. After all, she had a life and a husband of her own, and here was this crazy kid from her school who was blowing his mind on drugs, right before her eyes. She was simply trying to help him move on.

Fortunately, it worked. With nowhere else to go, the youth took her advice and enlisted in the Army right there in Phoenix. He was shipped off to Fort Lewis, Washington for basic training, hoping to escape from his increasingly crisis-filled home life and several legal issues in Kansas City.

His breakneck pace didn't change at first, but it only lasted a little while, as he couldn't avoid the disciplined atmosphere and forced accountability of military training. As it turned out, the new environment actually did the boy some good, clearing his head and his health… at least a little. With a uniform and a new haircut, he propelled into leadership as the platoon captain. He especially loved hearing the entire platoon cheer as the commanding officer brought him breakfast in bed, his prize for winning the first-place trophy in the camp's toughest obstacle course.

By the time he'd graduated from boot camp in late 1968, the new recruit discovered his girlfriend was pregnant back in Kansas City. He knew enough of his dad's conviction that, if you impregnate a woman, then you're responsible for her and the child's well-being.

Calling from the military base to her home in Kansas, he immediately asked his girlfriend, "Will you marry me, please?" This marked the start of a ruckus-filled wild ride, that began with his very romantic proposal from a phone booth 2,000 miles away!

As you can imagine, his head was spinning for days afterwards. He decided to continue his military training by becoming a paratrooper, which was much more exciting to him than being a simple rifleman or stateside soldier. To do that, he and his new bride knew they'd need to relocate to the Army's paratrooper/ranger training base in Fort Benning, Georgia.

After only a few days at the new school, he discovered that before he'd be able to experience the rush of actually jumping out of planes, he'd first have to spend weeks learning and practicing techniques in a hangar on the ground first.

After earning his "jump wings," he was sent for further specialized training as a "rigger" at Fort Lee, Virginia, pushing his skills further as he focused on precision vehicle, weaponry and heavy-equipment drops. At the same time, he mastered the precise folding and packing of parachutes for the entire crew, carefully inspecting chutes for damage before each jump.

That's why he often found himself back at Fort Benning talking to Esther, the elderly civilian on base who supplemented her retirement pension by putting her sewing skills to work for the Army. The young soldier knew the old woman was an experienced seamstress, and a classic southern Bible-thumper to boot.

He wasn't prepared for Esther's reaction when she'd found out that, in the space of just twelve months, the young recruit had graduated from high school, joined the army, gotten married and had a baby! The old woman knew he was still drinking heavily and chasing prostitutes, escaping to the notorious off-base party towns of Phoenix City, Alabama and Columbus, Georgia during his off-hours.

Calling him by the name stenciled over the shirt pocket of his green army fatigues, Esther looked him straight in the eye and demanded, "Hey Kornis, you gotta be born agin! Yer life's in a tumble, boy."

"You goin' to heaven or hell, Kornis?"

.

> Whoever is a believer in Christ is a new creation.
> The old way of living has disappeared. A new
> way of living has come into existence.
>
> *Paul, 2 Corinthians 5:17*

CHAPTER 2
PASSING THROUGH GEORGIA
ON THE ROAD TO HEAVEN... OR HELL?

Yes, it's true. In case you hadn't realized it, that crazy, mixed-up, wild-eyed soldier boy was me - Fred Kornis, Jr.

To be honest, I'm a little self-conscious and horribly ashamed of telling you details of the life I lived so long ago. This is mostly because it scares me when I look back at where my head was... where my heart was... and where the path I was on was leading me at full speed, way back then.

However, I'm reminded of the saying, "I wish I knew then what I know now," and I must tell you, I'm glad I've learned all I know now. Hopefully, you'll benefit from both my good and bad experiences. Although these experiences made me who I am today, I would never wish for those days to come back again.

If you see some of yourself in these stories, maybe you'll see a way out, too. Maybe you'll see a reason to continue down the path you're on, or maybe you'll see a glimmer of hope. Maybe you'll even see a whole rainbow of

27

possibilities.

I don't know what you'll take from this book, but I hope you'll find something here that helps you live the rewarding life you deserve.

Please know that everything you dream of is possible, and within your reach. To prove it, I'll tell you how a string of mysterious and unexpected things happened along the way through my early life of destruction, drugs and despair.

While there's no way I could have planned them all (believe me, I didn't plan *anything* in my early days), I'm convinced that our Creator put people and things in my path at just the right time. Everything was for me to find, recognize and use, as soon as I was ready for a greater life than I even knew was possible at the time.

That's the thing though, isn't it? Being able to recognize what's actually in front of you makes all the difference. Eventually, bit by bit, I'm learning to accept the Lord's guidance, when He sends me the choices that actually help my life and people around me the most.

Here's what I mean...

The wildest dancer

By the time I was finishing junior high school, I'd already established my reputation as a wild dancer, playing gigs as the lead singer in rock bands around the Kansas City area on weekends.

One day, as I was riding my bicycle along Delmar Street about two blocks away from my home in Roeland Park, Kansas, I passed a few teenagers hanging out on the sidewalk, with a neighborhood band practicing beside them. I recognized one of the girls, Janice, when she waved me over to meet a friend of hers.

"You've gotta see this guy dance, Barb, he's wild!" she said, as I laid my bicycle down on the sidewalk in front of Janice's house.

I immediately started movin' and groovin' to the music that filled the neighborhood, and all the kids around us were cheering and dancing. That's when I first laid eyes on Barb Mendelsohn, who was visiting her best friend.

We hung out together a few times after that, and began to feel a connection. I found out she was a year older than me and already in high school. We exchanged phone numbers to stay in touch.

I couldn't know it at the time, but Barb would later become a stabilizer in my life for over 50 years! (See what I mean about the Lord guiding our lives, despite us?)

The trouble was, as I entered the ninth grade at school, I had gotten all wrapped up in my music, and started coping with my anger by drinking plenty of alcohol and sniffing glue. Since my early childhood, my dad was always very physical, and he'd taught me boxing; he taught me to fight. He'd drive me to my limits all the time, sometimes pushing me until I cried.

It broke my heart. I guess he was trying to build endurance and something strong in me, but I never really understood that. I was intense and going full-speed-ahead all the time, always fighting and always in trouble. My mom had already left our home by that time, and I was definitely living on the edge all through my early years.

I immersed myself in music, always listening to rock and roll albums and trying to pantomime and imitate these new gods. Soon I was playing in neighborhood rock bands, which encouraged my introduction to marijuana.

By the 12th grade, I was a regular user, and was branching out into other drugs, especially LSD. The acid culture became my philosophy... well, mine and that of my so-called "friends" at the time. We would roll up dollar bills and snort powdered speed or coke up our noses.

We were telling ourselves, "Do your own thing and don't let anything stop you. The only thing that's true is whatever you think."

I can still hear one guy saying to me, "There's a big word for all this. It's called Relativism. But it means the same thing... nothing really matters."

As the music world became my life, so did the drug business. I was making money from both of them. It reached the point where some of the guys I hung around with carried guns in their cars, and we were attracting the attention of law enforcement agencies.

One night, as my friend Jim and I were doing drugs together, he giggled, "Hey, did you see the car parked across the street from the club?"

"Yeah, there was some dude sitting in it," I mumbled.

"It wasn't some dude, man." Jim's face went all serious. "That guy is with the FBI."

"Are you putting me on?" I asked incredulously. "Why the FBI?"

"Would you want the fuzz to stop us right now and shake down the car... and us?" Jim asked.

"All I got on me now is a couple of joints," I justified.

"That's enough, man. But if they found the loaded piece I got under the seat, we'd really have trouble."

I'd totally forgotten about the loaded gun Jim kept in the car, so now I was spooked. "How long do you suppose that Fed has been watching us?"

"The bartender at the club said he came in about a week ago, asking questions."

I started looking for a way out. "You know, I think I ought to travel," I said aloud.

"Hey, where to?" Jim wondered, a spark of interest in his eyes.

"California." I shot back instantly, "My mom and little sister Melody are out there in Santa Maria, you know, right near San Francisco."

"Hey, that's the best," Jim smiled. "Rock City, alright!"

"Yeah, I might see Hendrix, Joplin and the Animals," I told him. "Almost everybody who's big in rock hangs out there."

The threshold of pain

In 1967, during the peak of the flower-power scene in Haight-Ashbury when all the famous names in rock were playing at the *Fillmore West*, I went to live with my mother in Santa Maria. I enrolled in the local high school, and spent as much time as I could with people who were as much into the culture as I was.

One of my creepy new friends opened up a whole new way of thinking to me by saying, "It's good to expand your mind, but dropping acid and smoking pot aren't the only ways to break through the sensation barrier."

"Oh, like what else?" I prompted him.

"Like pain, man. You know, doctors talk about the threshold of pain. You know what they mean?"

"Yeah," I answered, "it's the point where a person actually starts to feel pain. I mean you might not feel the needle when there's only a little pressure on it, but the harder you press it in, the more you feel it. The threshold of pain is where it starts to hurt."

"You got it," creepy-guy nodded, "and for each different person, the threshold of pain is different."

This was totally new to me, so now I was curious. "Would you like to find out what yours is?" my friend continued.

"How?" I wondered eagerly.

"I got some cigars here," my mind-expanding partner smiled mischievously. "I'll light one and we'll lay it on your arm."

"Why not a cigarette?"

"Too hot, too quick," he informed me. "With a cigar, it takes longer. Now lay your arm out on the table."

At first, I didn't feel the burn at all. My friend continued to push the lit cigar into my bare flesh, to see how deep and how long my arm could withstand the burning embers!

"This is all in the interests of science," he explained. "Can you feel it burn?"

"Not yet. It feels warm, though," I replied.

"You're approaching the threshold, man. Do I smell burning flesh?"

"I don't know," I hesitated. "Maybe. Ouch, ouch! Okay, that's enough!"

"Hey, don't ruin the cigar, man!" he cautioned me. "I might want to use it again. Maybe somebody else will want to learn about *their* threshold of pain."

(I still have some scars I could show you, as permanent reminders of crazy experiments like that one.)

As soon as I'd finished my last year of high school in California, I headed back to Kansas City to get my diploma in my home town. But by that time, I was so disorganized by the drugs I'd been taking, I couldn't cut it as a musician anymore.

Back at home, my dad helped me buy a *Triumph Bonneville* motorcycle, with lots of chrome and a 650cc engine. One of my favorite movies was *Easy Rider* starring Peter Fonda, and I drove my bike like I was "born to be wild" (one of the big hit songs from the movie). The first day, I roared down the I-35 interstate at over 100 mph... and I started racking up moving traffic violations in no time.

One day, riding through downtown Kansas City, I lost control of my bike, trying to run away from a cop chasing me. I hit a telephone pole and bounced over an embankment. Swerving to avoid hitting a dump truck, I flew 30 feet in the air, landing against the back of a house. Within seconds, the bike was a mess, and my wrist was broken.

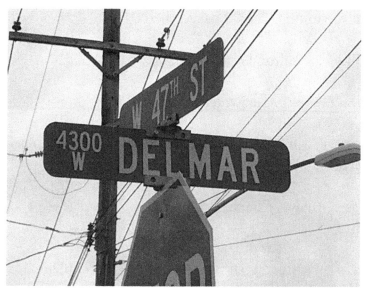

Dancing with Barbara for 50 yrs!

While I was in the hospital, I refused to sign the ticket as the police officer stood by my bedside. While I was cussing and yelling at the cop for hassling me in the hospital, I suddenly noticed my dad at the door. He looked broken hearted as he listened to his son's stupidity.

The next day, believe it or not, I went water skiing!

"Did you ever see anything as pretty?"

With the legal heat getting to be too much for me in Kansas City, I began thinking about going back to California. Paul and Scott, a couple of guys I knew, were immediately interested when I told them about my plans.

"Hey man, if you're really serious about going back out there, we could cut you in," they told me.

35

"Cut me in on what?" I asked them.

"A little agricultural enterprise," Paul hinted.

"I don't get it," I answered, a puzzled look on my face.

"You will tonight, when we show you High Acres," he smiled.

I was so naive. "Is that the name of the place?" I asked him.

"No, that's just what we call it," Scott explained. "It's almost as great as the poppy fields in *The Wizard of Oz*. See you tonight!"

Sure enough, I realized exactly what he meant, when I met them at a hidden field near Lawrence, Kansas later that night. "Did you ever see anything as pretty as all that 'grass' growing in the moonlight?" Paul grinned, proudly showing off his marijuana crop.

"Wow, how many acres of it have you got?" I asked, wide-eyed.

"Not acres," Paul corrected me, "but enough that we'll be here all night chopping it, and all day tomorrow drying it. Then we'll have to put it in bags."

Finally, I got the picture and said, "Now I understand. We'll sell the pot along the way."

"That's it, man. We're going to travel in style," said my new travel partners. "And at $10 a bag, we'll be going strictly first class."

"Alright!" I beamed, and eagerly spent the night curing fresh-cut grass in an oven, with Paul and Scott's guidance.

Within a few days, we headed out to California by way of Denver and Salt Lake City, selling pot in many of the towns along the way. We also traded some of our stash for speed and acid. You might say that helped to broaden the base of our clientele.

From there, we went first to San Francisco, then down to Los Angeles. I was getting more and more strung out, and lost track of how much of the drugs I was taking every day.

Now maybe I ought to go back a little, to explain the ways that God had been on my mind up to that point in my life. One night, back in Missouri, I was high on dope, and felt a terrible emptiness and confusion over romance and relationships. A heavy storm was brewing in the clouds above the house. Wearing nothing but my underwear, I ran out of the house and into the street.

On the grassy section of the median strip in the middle of the road, I stopped, laid flat on my back, and looked up at the stormy sky. Rain poured down on me as I lifted my hand to Heaven and shouted, "God, oh God!"

I was certain that God answered me when I cried out,

because a sudden and startling bolt of lightning struck the ground close to me at that spot in the median.

Later, in Los Angeles, I'd developed some sort of defiant attitude about death. In a large cemetery overlooking the sparkling lights of the city, I ran among the grave marker stones in the middle of the night. I had this strange experience that I was dodging the clutches of death, and the fingers of death were reaching up through the sod to grasp my ankles and bare feet.

It seemed so real to me that my heart nearly jumped out of my chest! (In fact, to this day, I still look down at my feet and don't know what parts of that experience were actually real.)

"What made you decide to join up?"

On the way home from my West Coast pot-bagging trip, I had the sudden urge to visit Nancy, my former high-school teacher, who was living in Phoenix, Arizona. When she saw the dazed look in my drug-dulled eyes, she sat me down and we talked about where my life was going.

By the end of our conversation, Nancy had the sudden feeling that I needed to break away from the destructive behavior that had taken over my days, and go straight.

With the local Army recruiting station nearby, she recognized that the military and the draft were symbols of everything my life needed. With Nancy's help, I went to enlist for boot camp.

The recruiter was ready to sign me up, and clearly said, "Don't misunderstand me. The Army wants you, Fred, but I'm curious... what made you decide to join up?"

"Well, partly being down on my luck." I told him. "I'm so broke, I had to break into a mission church last night and sleep on the floor. I'm also ashamed of all the hassle and hurt I've caused my family."

With encouragement and hope, he said, "Well, we'll see if we can get you a partial pay right away."

The recruiter assured me that the military would help, saying, "Army basic will sweat the dope out of you. Enlisting this way, you can choose what kind of an outfit you want to be in. Have you thought anything about that?"

"Yeah," I responded, "I want to be an Airborne paratrooper."

He raised his voice as his head snapped up to meet my gaze, and he laughed. "Airborne? Oh, you really *do* want to make a break with your old life!"

I was sent to Fort Lewis, Washington that same week for basic training. From there, I was scheduled to go to Fort Ord, California, so I called my girlfriend Barb from a phone-booth on base, to tell her of my new direction.

She was thrilled to hear that some of the dangerous life I'd been living was about to change. Then she casually mentioned, "Oh, by the way, I'm pregnant."

My head swirled. By my way of thinking, my responsibility was clear, and I already knew the code of conduct my dad had drilled into my head.

True to form, my mind was made up. I immediately asked Barb, "Will you marry me, please?" I know, what a romantic proposal from a phone booth in a bowling alley!

When I received my first weekend pass from the base about three months later, I went home to Kansas City, and married the girl I'd dated, on and off, for several years. The wedding was on Saturday, February 22, 1969 in her Aunt Sara and Uncle Harold Mendelsohn's living room. I had to be on duty in Fort Knox, Kentucky, the following Monday morning, so we had to drive straight through to make it in time.

I dragged my new wife there for our "honeymoon", and put her in a little 10-foot *rat's-nest* trailer we were able to rent near the base. No TV or radio. And since I had to be on duty all week, I couldn't even leave the base.

Needless to say, Barb and I had a really rocky beginning to our marriage!

In fact, that entire first year was pretty wild. I'd gotten totally wrapped up in the military life, especially after winning the trophy for my platoon in boot camp. I won first place on the obstacle course, too, pouring all my frantic energy into something constructive for a change.

Our daughter, Summer, was born later that year (you can probably guess the season!).

After basic training, I continued my military training at tank and wheeled-vehicle school, then immediately dove into training as a paratrooper at Fort Benning, Georgia.

From there, I specialized as a rigger, which is the person who is responsible for all the parachutes - folding and packing them for live use, as well as repairing and hanging parachutes for weapons, heavy equipment and precision vehicle drops. I found out it's quite a technical thing to drop vehicles from a plane, and when they release a Jeep from the sky with parachutes, the riggers are the people who handle that. I guess we would pray that we did it right.

I was usually working from an aircraft hangar at Fort Benning, Georgia, basically packing parachutes all day. Every now and then, our CO would pull a parachute from a pile, throw it to me and say, "Jump it." I'd have to go up in the airplane and jump, with a random parachute strapped to my back. Yes, it was a big risk to take, to make sure you're doing your job right!

Back at our makeshift home, Barb was patient and loyal. She allowed me to ignore her or mistreat her when I felt like it, and yet she was waiting for me when I'd come looking for her. By this time, I was pretty well off drugs, but I was still drinking all the time. Summer was still a baby, and Barb spent most of her time caring for her and taking care of our home.

"Shut up, you fool!"

To say I had no relationship with God wasn't true... it's just that we weren't on very friendly terms, as far as I was concerned. One drunken day, back in the city of Louisville, Kentucky, I saw a crowd gathered around, listening to a very tall man who was preaching on the street.

He spoke out boldly, saying, "One of the most beautiful words in the English language is *forgiveness*. Most of the time, though, if you want to find forgiveness, the place to look is in the dictionary between 'forfeit' and 'forlorn.'"

"Yet most of us need to be forgiven. We've probably broken the law more than once, and even if we haven't been caught, we suffer from guilt. We find it hard to even forgive ourselves, and it's often impossible to be forgiven by people we've hurt. We may tell ourselves, 'I'm no worse than other people,' but that doesn't really do away with our feelings of guilt."
"Yet it's possible to be forgiven. Not by the law, not by other people, but forgiven by God Himself."

As the man continued to speak, some people paused and listened.

"How can we be forgiven?" he continued. "By putting our trust in Christ as our Lord and Savior." The Bible says, 'Who can forgive sins but God only?' It also says this about Christ Jesus, 'In whom we have redemption through his blood, the forgiveness of sins, according to the riches of his grace...' "

As the street preacher spoke his truth, I worked my way through the small crowd until I stood right in front of him. Seeing my face distorted and ugly with anger, he surveyed the crowd and said, "Friends, the best news in all the world is this. If you believe in the Lord Jesus Christ, thou shalt be saved. That means forgiveness and eternal life."

Suddenly I heard another voice shouting back in protest - and it was mine!

"You loud-mouthed fool! Why don't you sit down and shut up? Nobody is going to listen to a crazy fanatic like you. Nobody is going to believe that crazy stuff. Shut up!"

The preacher was gentle and firm, speaking directly to me when he said, "Friend, the Bible says, 'That if thou shalt confess with thy mouth the Lord Jesus, and shalt believe in thine heart that God hath raised him from the dead, thou shalt be saved.'"

I started shouting at him in a threatening tone, "Shut up, you fool! Shut up! Shut up!"

For some reason, I felt a sense of relief or satisfaction with my argument, so I turned and stomped away down the sidewalk. I never found out who the street preacher was, and never saw him again. I simply went back to my barracks, and continued fumbling with my efforts to straighten myself out.

"Sounds great, doesn't it?"

With my hard drinking, I was kind of half-crazy. Some people would say I was *all* crazy. No wonder Barb began getting angry with me, especially after I was assigned to go to Fort Benning, Georgia for my airborne jump-school training.

I can still hear the tone in her voice asking, "Tell me something, Mr. Knievel, was that you who just rode up on a motorcycle?"

"Yeah, sounds great, doesn't it?" I answered, sheepishly. She knew something was up, and replied, "It sounds to me like an awful lot of money. Where did you get it?"

Stalling to avoid the question I hoped she wouldn't ask, I said, "The bike?"

"No, the money," she answered, pointedly.

"Well," I stuttered, "I, uh, traded something."

"What have *you* got to trade?" she snarled. "I can't think of anything but your Army issue uniforms... and maybe your soul."

"Very funny, Barb. What I traded was a car," I finally admitted.

"A car? But you don't own a car," she demanded.

"No, honey. But you do," I said, remembering that I had

"inherited" her car at our wedding. Since I didn't have a vehicle when we'd gotten married, we were using Barb's nice little Malibu to get around.

"What? You mean I *did* own a car!" Barb realized. "Fred Kornis, that's the dirtiest, most dishonest thing I have ever heard of. Here I am with our one-year old child, and you expect me to walk? Or worse yet, have us ride on the back of a motorcycle?"
I told her, "I've got a car for ya. It has electric seats and windows... and the whole car only costs $25!"

"Don't get so excited," I said, trying to calm my wife. But her last words rang out loud and clear... and I knew they were exactly true.

"Why not?" she fumed. "I know you've been stealing things from this house to sell them for liquor. Now it's my car! You want my advice? Go see a shrink. There's something wrong in your head!"

When I eventually calmed down from this conflict, I took Barb's advice to heart, but the Army doctor didn't help me. I was asking questions like, "Who am I? What is the ultimate? What is reality?" The analyst seemed so shallow to me, and I thought he needed help more than I did.

The next weekend, I went out walking in the country, trying to figure out some answers to the big questions swirling around in my brain. Crossing a railroad line, I turned and followed it, changing my gait as I walked to match the placement of the wooden ties.

As I stepped between the rails, with their polished edges gleaming in the moonlight, it seemed like they were swaying and surging all by themselves. You see, I had smoked and snorted so much dope over the years that I couldn't even trust solid objects to stand still anymore. My emotions and senses were all confused.

The steel rails seemed to keep swaying, and the green block signal almost a mile down the line flickered in the corner of my eye. Meanwhile, the voices from all my music heroes invaded my thoughts.

"Manic depressive," I started singing. "No, no that's wrong. Let's see. It goes like this... 'manic depression is a frustrating mess. Manic depression...' who cares? It's all the same." I started talking to myself as I sang. "Manic depression... hey, that's Jimi Hendrix's song! Sure, Jimi is dead. So is Janis Joplin. So is... aw man, they're all dead."

Before I could finish my thought, a real train blared its horn as it roared by me at full speed, breaking my hypnotic trance. I was shocked and scared, my heart pounding in my chest. "That was close," I said to no one in particular. "That was *way* too close."

My mantra

In the weeks that followed, I decided to try something new, hoping to put the pieces of my jumbled brain back in order. I started experimenting with TM, transcendental meditation, inspired by some literature a friend from home had sent me.

During my self-guided deep meditation sessions, I'd remember laying in our backyard as a child, looking up at the moon and stars with my dad. After witnessing the grand scale of the universe so far above me as a young boy, I'd often lay in bed in the dark, horrified, and thinking, "What if I did not exist?" or "What if I was nothing?"

"What if there wasn't me?" I'd ponder. "If I didn't exist?" The thoughts began haunting me again, because it was scary to imagine not existing or being nothing! I was 21 years old, and still wondering, "What is my meaning, what is my purpose? Why am I here? What is the meaning of life?"

Barb started to notice changes in my manner. "Fred," she pointed out, "all you do lately is sit and stare into space."

"I'm not sitting and staring," I explained. "I'm meditating."

"Oh, I don't know about you, Fred," Barb replied. "Last night you told me that from now on, you're not eating any meat and becoming a vegetarian. I think you've flipped."

My transcendental meditation phase continued with more and deeper experimentation. I had taken more LSD than most people took aspirins. I had snorted cocaine and speed with rolled-up dollar bills. I had also used to sniff glue to get a buzz. I was high for days and weeks at a time.

Through all of that, I still kept asking, "Who am I, where am I? What is the meaning?" I also kept a loaded pistol in my top drawer, mixed in with all my other drug paraphernalia, pornography, and suicidal thoughts in my head... just in case I didn't find an answer soon.

"Being 'saved' is impossible..."

My poor wife must have often thought, "What have I gotten into?" Until then, she'd enjoyed a pretty normal, seemingly perfect life. Barb's mom took care of three beautiful daughters, and her father was a hard-working, faithful Jewish man.

Now she'd left this idyllic, "perfect" life for me. I was one of three boys, raised in a single-parent home with no girls, no mom, no sisters... and we were wild as hell. While she was now married to me, I knew she often felt like she just wanted to go home. She was so loyal and faithful that she stuck by me through all it. Barb was naturally a home-body, but she kept going along with me in my military life.

True to form, I threw my heart and soul into paratrooper training, my new passion. Very quickly, the energy that used to go into crime and drugs and everything else went into learning how to survive in war, and jumping out of airplanes. As usual with me, it was all or nothing.

Within weeks, I'd advanced into training as a parachute rigger. I learned to set up precision parachute drops with weapons, tanks and heavy equipment, and mastered the skillful folding and packing of parachutes for our entire platoon.

I couldn't know it at the time, but God put a very special person in my path while I was there at Fort Benning.

On base, there was an elderly woman named Esther Calhoun, who was supplementing her retirement income by working as a seamstress for the Army. Whenever I discovered any of the chutes I was packing were ripped or torn, I would have to take them to her. She was responsible for sewing the silk and make them "jump ready" again.

We'd often talk when I dropped off another bunch of parachutes to get fixed each week. I could tell by her voice that she was a hillbilly from Georgia. To my ears, she couldn't really speak any English -- it sounded like she had marbles in her mouth when she talked with her down-home Southern accent.
I would see Esther maybe every day or every other day, and I couldn't stand her because she was a "religious freak." She was one of those old Baptist women; a gray-haired widow who was always trying to talk to me about the Lord. Meanwhile, I was still drinking hard, and feeling suicidal more days than not.

Suddenly this woman was in my workplace, and she kept talkin' about Jesus. "Kornis, you need to be born agin, boy. You goin' to Heaven or hell Kornis?" she'd say.

I thought, "What the hell is this dumb woman talking about, she doesn't even speak English. What the hell?"

When she laid it on me like that, I thought, "You gotta be kidding!" I thought anybody with that kind of accent had to be stupid.

Still, Esther would often tell me, "Kornis, whatever confusions you have, remember this one thing. God loves you no matter what." Even though I usually thought of her as one of those crazy Bible-thumpers, I knew she had a good heart, with pure love coming out of her piercing blue eyes.

I decided to just swallow my pride ...

I found out somewhere along the line that Esther was a widow and she lived alone. At the same time that I was repulsed by her, I was also attracted to her. "Here's this female with affection," I thought in the back of my mind. "Here's this woman who cares about me and, oh, I've never had enough of a mother's hug and touch." I was torn by the paradox of feeling repulsed, and yet feeling completely drawn to her.

On a Saturday morning in 1970, the 11th day of July, I decided to swallow my pride, and go to her house to help her with some home repairs and cut the grass. As I sat in her living room across from her, I couldn't turn away again from her piercing blue eyes looking at me. They were so full of love and peace that I didn't have myself. I was still so tormented by my own conscience, and my own agonies in life.

Esther penetrated me with questions. "Kornis," she said. She never called me Fred, never once in her life, because on my green Army fatigues, only my last name was sewn above the pocket on the front. She said, "Kornis, what's your life all about?"

I tried to make sense of everything I'd lived through up to that point, saying, "Well, rock music, heavy drugs, some dealing, and now meditation and my new family. I've also been thinking a bit lately about religion, I guess."

Esther put all the emphasis on one person as she said, "What about the Lord Jesus Christ?"

As I struggled with my own world view of religion, she continued. "Religion is not at all the same thing, Kornis. We can't be saved by a religion, a church, a philosophy, a set of rituals, or even by doing good deeds."

"Well if that's true," I reasoned, "then being 'saved,' as you say, is impossible."

"With God all things are possible," she countered. "The need is to recognize our guilt, to know that we're sinners, and then to trust in Jesus Christ *himself* for forgiveness."

Esther was speaking deep into my heart. Her eyes seemed to look directly into my very soul.

"You sound like a street preacher I heard once in Louisville," I said, embarrassed at the memory.

"Did you like what he said?" she asked, pressing the issue.

"No, I think I spit on him," I sheepishly admitted. "I was pretty drunk."

"Well, the preacher could take it, Kornis. He was speaking for the Lord Jesus Christ, and for the sake of Jesus, and for your soul. That preacher was probably able to enjoy your spitting" (Isaiah 53).

"They did that to Jesus?" I replied, beginning to see the light.

"They did," Esther nodded. "But of course, it had been described by the prophet Isaiah more than seven centuries before it even happened."

"Really? Prophesied, like predicting the future?" I was thinking out loud.

"Let me read you from my Bible what it says," she announced, as she reached for the well-worn Bible on the table beside her.

"You know that book pretty well, don't you?" I asked.

"I read it every day," she told me. "Here, here, listen. 'I gave my back to the smiters, and my cheeks to them that plucked off the hair. I hid not my face, from shame and spitting.' That's from Isaiah 50:6."

I looked at her in disbelief. "That was written seven hundred years before it happened?"

"Of course," she affirmed. "The Old Testament is full of prophesies of the coming Messiah that were fulfilled in Jesus."

"What do you mean by the word *saved*, Esther?" I asked, a little hesitation in my voice.

"I mean forgiven by the grace of God, washed in the shed blood of Christ. 'By grace are ye saved through faith,'" she recited from Ephesians 2:8-9. "Trust in Jesus for the gift of eternal life."

"So, what about you, Kornis?" she challenged me. "What about heaven? What about hell? What about your life?"

Right there in her living room, I don't know how these medical scientists, doctors, professionals and all these know-it-alls would explain it, but I broke.

My conscience, my will and my heart broke wide open, and I started bawling and sobbing. I couldn't think, I couldn't argue, and I couldn't stop. I just started weeping uncontrollably in the room with Esther.

I think she was scared to death. She must have thought, "Oh my God, he's having a nervous breakdown."

As tears flowed from my eyes, it was like Esther had disappeared. Suddenly, there was nobody else in that room with me. I was sitting somewhere out in eternity, in the presence of God Himself. I sobbed and sobbed and moaned, and it came out of me like Niagara Falls. All the pain from my childhood, my mother's abandonment, abuse, and guilt - all of it poured out of my soul.

I don't know how long it went on for, it could have been an hour, or maybe just half that. The next thing I knew, Esther had her hand on me. She's was kind of whispering to me, "Kornis... Kornis, Kornis. You're saved now. You're saved. You're saved."

I was still thinking, "What the hell does 'saved' mean?" I didn't know about being saved. I just knew I wasn't religious. She said, "That's okay, you're saved now."

As I got my breath back and pulled myself together, she basically explained to me that I'd become a true believer, that I had been born again. Well, I didn't know what that meant. I'd never read the Bible. I didn't understand those terms and all those religious words.

I just knew that my heart had shattered. I knew that I'd called upon God. I couldn't explain it with religious words, but I had experienced something divine. I had become a *new creation* (2 Corinthians 5:17; Galatians 1:11-12).

Fred and Esther Calhoun (1995)

"Who do you think you are, Mr. Clean?"

For the following week or two, things went crazy. When I went home, Barb thought I was nuts. She thought, "Oh no, another drug!" She was sure I was crazy before, and now I was religious-crazy... and she didn't want anything to do with it.

Barb was scared to death of me, and I feared her. To my new understanding, I thought she was full of the devil.

A popular TV jingle at the time sang, "Mr. Clean can clean your whole house and everything that's in it." The song went with an animated ad for a household cleaner, and when you opened the bottle, this genie would pop out and fly around the house. Your house would be sparkling clean, and then he'd go back in the bottle.

Barb hit me with the question, "Who do you think you are, Mr. Clean?"

She asked this, because when I came home, I went from black to white. I've always been an extremist, so if I was going to be a Christian, I was going all the way. There was no middle of the road. Be one or the other. Get in or out. After all, if you're jumping out of an airplane, you don't hesitate. I jumped right into things feet first, and everything else to follow.

I think I waited more than two weeks for my first Bible to come in the mail. I'd go every day to Esther's church, knocking on the door and saying, "Did my Bible come yet? I want a Bible!" In the meantime, I went out and found one of those hotel Gideon Bibles, and I started reading that instead.

It was supernatural. Really...totally supernatural!!

Meanwhile, Barb was watching me turn our world upside down, with her half-Jewish background becoming more and more significant in my new life. The more I read from the Bible, the more I started to get all those Biblical references about the Jewish people, which just set me on fire.

When she saw me throw out all my drug paraphernalia, break up my rock albums, and burn my pornography collection, Barb thought for sure I was crazy. A few weeks later though, she also put her trust in Christ, at a Navigators Bible Study group for ladies!

We were still together, with a shared bond that was now tighter than ever. Good thing too, because it wasn't long before my deployment orders came through in September from the Army. I was being assigned to the 173rd Airborne Infantry, as my force-fed introduction to the Vietnam war – the war from hell!

They'd booked me to leave before the end of the month, flying me right into a test of my new faith that would shake me to the core.

"Good morning Vietnam!"

> "God's Word is living and active. It is sharper than any two-edged sword and cuts as deep as the place where your soul and spirit meet, the place where your joints and your Morrow meet. God's Word judges a person's thoughts and intentions. No creature can hide from God. Everything is uncovered and exposed for him to see. We must answer to Him."
>
> *Hebrews 4:12-13*

CHAPTER 3
SPIRITUAL HOSPITAL

When I broke down in Esther's living room near the base at Fort Benning, I had no idea what was happening inside my head. I just knew that my heart broke.

I knew that I'd called upon God, and even though I couldn't explain it with religious words, I had experienced something divine. Nowadays, we call it a conversion, a change, salvation, or being born-again. But I don't give a flip what you call it, I just knew I'd felt a change.

You know, all these religious people try to give you a stinkin' formula, but I've never swallowed all the religious rituals, I've just lived in reality.
Up to that point, the reality was that my new marriage was off to a really rocky start. I had issues with drinking, anger, violence, and honestly, I was reckless.

But now we had a baby, and the whole thing of being a man, being responsible and being grown up needed to take a front seat in my life.

At the same time, I'd started spending more time at Esther's church. Pastor John Rigby was a fiery, red-headed preacher, and at the beginning, I hated his guts. Remember, before my conversion, I was a pure, total relativist with a sad, funny way of looking at the world. As far as I was concerned, the only thing you can be absolutely sure of, is that there are no absolutes.

After all, that's the way I was raised, with music like, "Sha-la-la, live for today." I was living by the credo, "Don't worry about tomorrow... and consequences and absolutes don't matter." The trouble is, that doesn't work in mathematics, or in the law of gravity... or in life itself. There *are* absolutes.

At that point in my life, I still didn't believe it. If anybody had an opinion, particularly about Heaven or Hell, or God, I was on attack mode. Remember the street preacher near Fort Knox, Kentucky that I cussed out when I was drunk?
Now suddenly, I'm that same kid who was invited into this church, listening to this old, red-headed southern preacher, Brother John Rigby, talk about absolutes. My whole being was so repulsed. I was thinking that guy was sick, and that I would kill him if I could, just to shut him up.

Learning to live in my new skin

That was how I was feeling *before* I'd had that supernatural experience with Esther in her home, where I became a real believer. After that transformation, everything changed for me. My heart was softer. I was still learning to live in my new skin, and I came to love Brother John.

I soon realized he loved the Bible and he loved God. In fact, I'd never been around anybody like him before. I'd only been around the skeptics and the bar-room theologians. You know, the kind of people who'd say things like, "Can God make a rock big enough He can't pick up?"

Pastor John Rigby was the guy who'd pointed Barb and me in the right direction. Our time at Fort Benning, when Barb and I'd gotten started, was the first real experience in our whole lifetime of anything called "church."

While I was initially repulsed by that religious stuff, it was there where we found real love. People encouraged us and loved us, just the way we were. It was a kind of genuine sincerity that we couldn't deny! Despite the system, the love there was real.

That was why we'd asked Brother John to baptize us and to get us our first study Bible. He'd ordered a classic edition called a Scofield Reference Bible, which cost about $50 at the time. So that was how I'd gotten started. I began to really appreciate Scripture, and wanted to learn the Bible from start to finish.

I'd be up half the night reading it, feeling like God was over my shoulder, whispering in my ear. It was really eerie, but it felt very real.

In September of 1970, my new orders had come through from the Army. I was assigned to fly out with my unit, the 173rd Airborne Infantry, to Vietnam. I ended up involved in both Medivac activities and a drug rehabilitation center for the GI's. The center was called *The Sky House,* and it was the first drug rehab program in our unit. I'd felt I was going to "be a missionary in Vietnam, paid for by *Uncle Sam,*" but my perspective was about to take a major hit. My newfound Christian beliefs would also be tested right along with it.

When God turned me upside down and sent me off to Vietnam, it was like He knew I needed to step into that environment. The Christian world calls it *discipleship* when you learn about and grow in your faith.

It was like He was saying, "Okay, if you want to get started in this new life, I'm going to send you into gross, unthinkable warfare, so you can really go deep on whether you're ready to take this Christianity thing seriously."

"Life is warfare"

The horror of my Vietnam war experience was virtually a personal trial by fire, that absolutely affected my heart for the rest of my life. That's why even today, when I stand in these religious buildings in front of a congregation with all of their rituals (and they have everything…their

T's crossed, their I's dotted, and everything's "perfect"), I get frustrated. I think, "You know, life is not all this cutesy little religious stuff. Life is warfare, and life is messy."

As a Medivac paratrooper, with helicopters and people getting killed all around me, I was living in the middle of a hell I'd never imagined. Seeing the most gruesome things in Vietnam, I often wept, crying out to God, "Why God? Why, God? Why all this horror, all this evil?"

War is hell, and life is war...

Fortunately, I wasn't alone in my misery. There were three of us working together in a place north of Danang called LZ English. Henry Brooks, an African-American from North Carolina, and Glenn Arnett, who now lives in Alabama, had become my soul brothers during that time.

Surrounded by the tragic day-to-day terror of war, we had to come to grips with the idea that, "Our world is full of evil, and we can't blame God. If you live by faith, there are many mysteries we will never understand" (Duet. 29:29).

That was a big wrestling point for all of us to deal with as we were doing our job, picking up injured guys with their body parts blown to pieces. I soon realized it was tough carrying a man on a stretcher, with guns blazing all around us, trying so hard to see our way back to the chopper with tears in our eyes.

Henry and Glenn had really gotten me into the Bible while we were in Vietnam. We'd do our own little Bible studies in between mortar attacks coming in, and we always kept our Bibles close by. (I still have my Bible to this day, even after it was soaked after a week of monsoon storms). We would read aloud to each other, right in the middle of that war zone.

My two Army buddies also gave me a great love for *all* books. Through them, I'd begun to hear names I'd never heard before, like C.S. Lewis, Charles Spurgeon, D.L. Moody, and Francis Schaffer. Digging deeper into books and education, I suddenly had the most unquenchable appetite to learn more! Soon, a man named George Verwer would also add fuel to this fire.

Proud of my stupidity

All the way through high school, I'd never read a book, and I was actually proud of myself for avoiding them. I would laugh at people and say, "Ha ha ha, I got out of high school and never had to read a book! Ha ha ha!" I guess I was proud of my stupidity. Now, suddenly, I'd realized that there was a universe of wisdom out there.

It was incredible to witness how, day after day in Vietnam, God helped us to be effective. We saw His Word and His spiritual disciplines affect our entire area. That's why, whenever possible, I would distribute small Bible booklets, translated into the Vietnamese language, to local people in the villages.

Finally, after the longest eight months I'd ever experienced in my young life, I found out I'd be able to go home in May of 1971. The CO told me I could possibly earn a Silver Star if I stayed until August, but he also gave me the choice to get out early. The Silver Star recommendation was primarily because of a "Cobra" helicopter shot down in front of us, and we'd guarded the pilot until he was rescued.

I told them flat out, "Are you kidding? Send me home now!" Since Barb had just given birth to our baby boy in February, I wanted to get home to meet him!

So, rather than take the chance of staying in the war zone and getting killed for a silver star on my chest, I chose to be discharged and sent home in May of 1971. I was ready to get re-acquainted with Barb, my daughter Summer and our new son, Jeremy.

Barb had been staying with her sister in their Kansas City apartment while she was pregnant. As soon as I arrived home from 'Nam, we moved into one of those low-income HUD apartments, on a hill called Mill Street in

Kansas City, Kansas. I don't think it lasted but three or four months before I was in another whirlwind.

My "spiritual parents" to the rescue

As a newly returned war veteran, I had access to the GI Bill from the government, so we started looking at colleges in Kansas and Missouri for me to go back to school. Unfortunately, none of them panned out.

But then Brother John Rigby, the pastor I'd met through Esther Calhoun at the time of my big spiritual awakening, called me from Columbus, Georgia about that time. He and Esther were like my *spiritual parents*, and I had always stayed in touch with Esther and her church group. She and Brother John recommended that I apply to Trinity College in Florida. He was on the board of directors there, and said, "If you want to go to Trinity College, I can get you into that school."

I felt like it was all a good connection, so when I was accepted, we pulled the plug in Kansas City, and made the move down to Florida. I was impressed that this was the school Billy Graham had graduated from, and that they'd taught him the Bible!

(I'm still in touch with Brother John's widow, Margie, even now. Believe it or not, as I'm writing this, we just received a check in the mail from her for a special donation to our organization, HIM. The connection still goes on today.)

Finding our way to Florida

We arrived in Dunedin, Florida just in time for the start of the school year. Barb and I lived with our two small children in many different places and apartments during the first few years. I'm not sure we'd ever been to Florida before that, and it was out of the clear blue sky that we'd decided to move there.

You can't hide who you really are

Right off the bat at Trinity college, it was hard for me to hide who I was as a person. That's always been true for me because I'm just kind of out there, in your face.

Amazingly, I ended up being the class president at Trinity for three years straight! That was a pretty amazing thing for me. I think it was because I was different and transparent. I wasn't the typical churchy kind of kid; I was kind of natural, and obviously *off-the-street*. It seemed that everybody either liked it or hated it.

From the very first week, I started studying. My favorite professor was a guy named Dr. E.C. Bragg, a renowned expert in systematic theology. As the primary theology professor at Trinity, he'd taught Billy Graham nearly two generations earlier, so it felt a bit profound to sit under a professor like him.

Another favorite was Dr. Ypma, who taught all the gospels, like the book of John. I think he was from Scotland, and he thrilled me with that Scottish brogue of his. It was exciting to hear every sentence, and he spoke with such drama! We were in awe, and captivated by the sound of his voice.

Fueling my fire

One course I was really passionate about was taught by Colonel Charles Massey, who had been a chaplain in the Army. He was focused on psychology and communication, which I really loved. In fact, I couldn't hardly walk down the street without talking to somebody next to me. I believed in communication so radically. Plus, I was attending his technical class with psychology, communication theory, and practice, and it really fueled my fire.

We also had a great pastor named Dr. Gordon Cross, who taught Christology, which was the life of Christ. He was such a godly man that he almost gave you the creeps. He was so holy - the way he carried himself, his posture, his face, the way he dressed. It was like he was from another world.

As a young student, I looked at all these different professors, each with a different personality, different presentations, and a different presence. They were all pretty cool, and had tremendous influence on an eager young guy like me. Funny thing is, I couldn't really name a "least favorite" professor. Because I was so hungry and excited about learning for the first time in my life, I loved soaking up wisdom, life, and everything around me.

Even when a course was tough to get through, but you knew it was required, you disciplined yourself to get through it. That's part of what you must do to get to the finish line… like it or not.

Spiritual Hospital

For someone in my "broken" condition, I've always considered Trinity College was my *spiritual hospital* for five years. After all, it was like an emotional, spiritual and physical hospital for my recovery from LSD, drugs, crime, PTSD, sin, and all the perversion I'd had in my life.

I still felt tremendous guilt, going back to when I was five years old and all the way through to my young adult life. I'd caused a lot of trouble and a lot of damage. I had been angry and immoral. I'd hurt many of the people around me, and caused them pain. I was so intense, and I was dangerous emotionally and physically.

In fact, I didn't find out until almost 20 years later, when I went to counseling with Barb, that a psychologist diagnosed me with something called IED -- *Intermittent Explosive Disorder.* In the big encyclopedia that psychologists use, this is a behavior disorder where the person has explosive outbursts of anger and violence, often to the point of rage. In my case, maybe it was from a childhood trauma, or it could have been partly in my DNA. Obviously, my Vietnam tour just added gas to the fire that really put me over the edge.

I was intensely enraged deep down, and my anger was often out of control. In hindsight, I realize that this is part of the amazing kaleidoscope of my life. God was dealing with me inside, in ways I didn't even realize while they were happening to me. Thank God for the doctors and counselors who've helped me along the way! I pray my kids also understand the miracle of my life.

"I don't want to be a Slick Willy"

Have you ever had a time when you felt you didn't know what you're doing, and you were living by the seat of your pants? At Trinity, I was usually flying along; somewhat of a loose cannon. I can always remember that we would have these chapel services, where all the students would gather three to five times a week and listen to guest speakers.

One guest speaker was Colonel Harlan Sanders. Remember, the chicken guy? Well, he was good friends with W.T. Watson, the president of Trinity, so he'd come in to speak to us.

We would also have all these great "mega-pastors," like Oswald J. Smith of the *Peoples Church* in Toronto, Canada, along with other authors coming in who were famous and super-professional. And with each speaker's presentation, I always remember doing this weird thing afterwards.

After the chapel was dismissed, and everyone was scattering and going to their rooms or back to class, I can remember I had this weird feeling in my heart. I would go around the corner, underneath a flight of steps, and get on my knees, all by myself. I'd say, "God, please don't let me be a professional. I don't want to be a *Slick Willy*."

In my mind, if you wore a coat and tie, or if you had the alphabet next to your name like a doctor, a professor, or a big shot, you were a professional... and I hated that. I had come off the street, where I didn't believe in the system, and now here I was in the middle of that same system, surrounded by all of these people!

In my own simple way, I prayed, "I don't know what you're going to do with me, God. I don't know where I'm headed for the rest of my life, but I never want to be a 'professional.' I just want to be a normal person, a regular guy, just like Jesus."

Most Christian colleges offer degrees for Pastors, Assistant Pastor, Music Director, Children's Education or missionaries. I never fit into any of those "boxes," but praise the Lord, God is so creative, and He had other plans for me.

Even today, I look around in wonder. I realize I've lived with a whole lot of rejection from many of the *scribes and Pharisees,* because I prayed when I was 22 years old, not to ever be super-slick and perfect. Yet because of that prayer, I've been able to reach tens of thousands of people, who'd never listen to those "slick willies" for a second. It's like God answered my prayer, and always kept me humble and a little rough around the edges for that reason.

Isn't it funny to see how things turn out, to see that, sometimes, you really do get what you wish for? There's an old expression, "Be careful what you wish for... you might get it!"

As it turned out, truer words were never spoken. I soon found a new life's journey opening up for me, partway through my time at Trinity. I don't believe for a second that it was "blind luck." I believe God's hand plopped the next phase of my career right into my lap... but for a price I would struggle to pay!

> "But you will receive power when the Holy Spirit comes to you. Then you will be my witnesses to testify about me in Jerusalem, throughout Judea, and Samaria, and to the ends of the earth."
>
> *Luke, Acts 1:8*

CHAPTER 4
THREE KIDS AND A WASHBOARD ON THE BUS TO... WHEREVER

A few months after starting my second year of classes at Florida's Trinity College in the fall of 1972, I was anxious to get Barb and our kids into a place where we could afford to live. I was fired up about the prospect of taking *mission trips*, and we were already planning one for the following summer.

My gung-ho brain went into overdrive, and I'd come up with an answer that would be just what we needed. It had just enough of an unorthodox twist that I knew it would suit me perfectly!

I had run across an old 1951 school bus that had been made into a camper, and found out I could buy it for only $2500. During Christmas break, Barb and I moved out of the house we were renting, and decided we'd live in the school bus to save money. Of course, we had three children at the time, including our newborn daughter, Faith, who'd just arrived the previous November.

I, met a fellow student named Leslie Miller, a

transplanted Canadian guy who owned an orange grove near Tampa, and he offered to let us park my school bus on the property next to his house. It seemed like the perfect way to have a "home of our own", and to reduce our expenses at the same time.

So the five of us moved into the small school bus, and Leslie let us hook up a hose to his outdoor faucet for water, along with an extension cord to the house for power. We lived there for a semester, and were planning to drive the bus as our *mobile home* for the scheduled summer mission trip to Mexico. We were both eager to move out with the Gospel.

By that time, people were getting really worried about Barb and our three kids, thinking that I was a little bit extreme. But I wasn't going to leave her without a modern dishwasher or something like that... so I bought Barb one of those old-fashioned scrub-boards and a tub to do our laundry! I can't tell you how *not* excited she was.

I know it sounds a little crazy now, but we were excited and sincere about our new ministry coming together. Our eagerness to take on the world made us believe we could get through anything.

In fact, even before springtime rolled around, Mr. Gung-ho (me) was ready to drop out of school and go to the mission field immediately. I was thinking, "Why waste my time? The world's going to hell! I ain't got time for this school stuff!"

Fortunately, some wise, gentle people, including Bill Bright, founder of Campus Crusade for Christ, kept telling me, "No, no, you need a foundation, you need an education. Don't be too anxious."

With an almost-four-year-old, a twenty-two-month-old, and a one-month-old baby crammed into the tiny quarters of our camper-bus, we somehow made it all work. I admit it wasn't fun all the time, actually many times it was quite challenging, but both Barb and I have always believed we are better off for such experiences.

We lived between the homes of two other students and their families on the orange grove, which was an hour outside of Tampa. I drove with them to school every morning, and in the midst of the bumper to bumper traffic, I would hold up CEF visual pictures and signs to the other glancing drivers next to us. Some would smile, and others looked scared to death.

Barb had a good time getting together with the wives and their kids, so it was like our own little private community. The kids were able to play outside in a huge yard, with plenty of space between us and our nearest neighbors, and it was really good. Except for the fire ants, that is.

Do you know what fire ants are? They are big ants that bite you mercilessly, creating a burning sore on your skin. We soon discovered that they're drawn to the sweetness of the orange trees. They create anthills that look more like big mountains all over the ground.

Unfortunately, whenever our son Jeremy was playing outside, the ants would crawl up his legs and bite him all over, leaving an unbearable rash of fire that was horrible for our two-year-old son. He loved to play outside and explore, but it seemed that he always found the biggest anthill to play in first!

Still, overall, we loved living on the orange grove, enjoying the freedom and having close friends nearby. It was a good six months. We were even able to join the migrant workers, picking fruit to make some extra money.

Meeting my first mentor at Trinity

With the big pieces of my student life in place, and our complete faith that the little things would soon fall into place behind them, I put all my energy into my studies at Trinity. Along with a full course load, I made sure to attend events when the faculty invited guest speakers to come in and share their real-world wisdom.

During one of the events that semester, I met someone who would change my heart forever, shaping and accelerating my missionary career well beyond my wildest hopes.

George Verwer is a prolific author, and he's the founder of the mission agency called *Operation Mobilization*. OM is one of the largest short-term mission agencies in the whole world. George led the organization with the help of his partner, Ray Eicher, in India. At any given time, they've had over 4,000 people out on mission fields around the world.

George and Ray spoke at Trinity early in the school year, and brought with them books to distribute, a method which was always at the core of the OM ministry. This got me addicted to reading books, to satisfy my unquenchable appetite for wisdom and ideas. Remember, I was still straightening out my LSD-fried, hallucinogenic brain, and George's books showed me a way to put the pieces back together.

As I was still trying to get back to reality, the books George Verwer shared gave me "the missionary bug" that day. I was inspired by Ray Eicher, who had even given up his US citizenship to become an Indian citizen, and was living his entire adult life in India. The whole idea of *Operation Mobilization's* approach and dedication to global ministry seized my imagination, and I wouldn't let it go.

That night, my mind raced with Verwer's stories of the people and needs he'd encountered around the world. On an impule, I went and woke him up at four o'clock in the morning to talk. He was staying in a trailer at a place called D and D Missionary Homes, in Saint Petersburg. So I knew he was not far from where I lived, and I had a million questions to ask him.

You see, after I'd heard George speak, my mind was reeling with the thought, "You have to be kidding. This guy is more radical than me. That's impossible!" I couldn't sleep that night because I was so fired up.

Turning his words over in my mind, I reasoned that if what he said was true, then most of us in America were possibly absolute fools. Why weren't we engaged, intentional and deliberate about reaching people who have never had a chance?

That was my first contact with a concept that I've lived by all my life since then...

"As long as there are millions who have never heard and that don't have an opportunity, how can I give all my time, attention and resources to the people around me that have all the opportunities and resources possible?!?"

You can find any answer you need

I realized that, here in the Western world, we are all gluttons for information. We have it all. I don't care if you're a Christian, a raging atheist, a pervert, a pagan, or whatever, if you want to go to church, it's here. You can also open a Bible and read it openly here. You can find any answer you need in the Bible...and it's at your fingertips.

However, that's not the case in India, Pakistan, Bangladesh, and so many other places throughout the developing world. Very few of the world's people have any of these opportunities, that we so often take for granted.

Sitting with Verwer at four in the morning, I also discovered what connected me to this man that was so undeniable. George Verwer was vulnerable with me, in ways no big-shot leader had ever been. He was open about his battles with doubts, lust, and pornography through the years. In my mind, having struggled with many of the same temptations and destructive experiences in my own life, I said to myself, "Wait a minute. This guy is real."

That's why, after waking him up in the middle of the night to say, "Hey George, what's the deal?" I knew he was no "Sunday-morning church-club guy." That's when I realized, "You know what? I can survive!" I was just 23 years old when I met George Verwer and I thought, "If this crazy radical can survive and be successful, I can do it, too!"

Taking on the challenge in Mexico

With a burning passion and a direction that I knew was right for me, I threw myself into my studies more than ever.

Remember, I'd already picked up the school bus to live in while I went to school, so I'd planned to gas it up and drive my family to OM's *mission base* in Mexico for the summer.

The trouble was, the more I looked into its condition, the more I realized there was no way we could use the bus as our mobile home for the trip. The tires were worn to threads, and the brakes didn't work. The engine would barely run long enough to power the vehicle across the driveway, let alone go on a cross-country trip! Ok, so my "visionary" style still needed time to mature!!

As you can probably guess by now, nothing was going to stop me. As soon as Trinity's classrooms closed for the summer, Barb and I piled our three children into my little Opel Cadet, and headed off for a fact-filled orientation conference put on by *Operation Mobilization* at Knox Presbyterian Church in Toronto, Canada.

From there, they sent nearly all the thousands of conference devotees out in teams, to various destinations all around the world. Barb and I chose to spend part of that summer in Mexico. We deepened our relationship with OM, as we ministered to that country's poverty-stricken people for the six weeks we were there. Dick Griffin was the Mexico director, and Jose Barrios mentored us in this cross-cultural work.

Squeezing a 4-year degree into five

Returning to Trinity after that first summer's eye-opening mission trip, the concept of, "Go go go!" got hold of me. I'd memorized the last words in Matthew 28, in which Jesus said, "*Go* into all the world, and share the good news with every creature. I'll be with you always."

It's been said that big doors swing on little hinges... and those two little words, *go* and *all*, became the hinges that would open the world to me. "*Go* into *all* the world"... those two little words took hold of my heart, and I started going.

I found I could start a conversation and share the teachings of Jesus with anybody, anywhere. I'd stand in front of grocery stores and say, "Do you know Jesus as our Lord? Here's a little booklet." For me, there was such an urgency about the "lostness" of humanity.

I'm sure plenty of people thought I was crazy. Actually, most of the verbal attacks came from religious people, especially if I wasn't a member of their particular denomination. But I kept moving though - in my radical way, from one extreme to another. I was conscious of going from suicide, drugs, immorality and everything else I'd endured, to going out and sharing my faith with other people. I witnessed to others, sharing the real changes and the reality of peace growing in my life and in others' each day.

At the same time, I was trying to get clear of the whole *Post Traumatic Stress Disorder* thing, with dark feelings that continued to cloud my mind. I think some form of PTSD had always been mixed up in my world, from my early childhood all the way through to my return from Vietnam (Jeremiah 17:9).

Verwer describes life with just four M's

One of my dark sides, that I've constantly been aware of and struggled with for years, is immorality. I've been filled with not only anger, but with lust, since even the days of my childhood. Knowing this, I believe it's a miracle that I've survived.

That is why I've come to realize that life is **MESSY**. My life is messy, and like you and everyone else, I need **MERCY**. I don't deserve anything, but it is comforting to know that always and everywhere, life is a **MIRACLE**.

81

It's all a miracle, and that's part of the everlasting **MYSTERY** that only Heaven will reveal (Deuteronomy 29:29). (You can read George Verwer's book <u>Messiology</u> for more on this idea.)

Remember, when it comes to life, you really don't know the whole plan, you are only seeing one part of that plan. It's only when you see the whole picture that you see the beauty of it. It's just like with a kaleidoscope, you can't see the whole, big picture when you're close-up; you're only seeing a small part of the beauty when you examine just a single piece.

God's kaleidoscope

This kaleidoscope, when God looks at everything in the world, the universe and the heavens above, is beautiful. All those broken pieces merge together into a wonderful image that reveals their beauty, like pulling back a curtain.

I believe it all becomes so clear when you look through the lens of the Bible and eternity. If we only see this world up close, through the tiny window of "today," the picture can never be complete. We have to take a bigger perspective to see it all from an eternal point of view. *Eternity* is real.

Eternity is our "ace in the hole." When you think about it, this is absolutely inspiring. Eternity offers us so many thoughts, reflections, feelings, possibilities, and hope that will endure anything this world brings us. That is beautiful!

Working towards my graduation from Trinity

As my graduation from Trinity College approached, it felt like the grand triumph of a great adventure for me. Esteemed Trinity alumnus Billy Graham spoke the keynote address, and inspired all of us to go out and spread the Word of God. All the years of studying and exploring theology by day, and working part-time jobs at night, were about to pay off.

To support our family, one of my part times jobs was cutting grass for retired people around Tampa and Clearwater. I had set up *Maranatha Lawn Service* with my partner Glen Speed, from Maine, and we spent many hours mowing together.

Plus, I worked in a mobile home factory in Florida, and then got a job with a contractor named George Gool, whom I'd met at Christ Community Church. I was doing home construction for him, and helped him build four houses. George ended up being a key person in my life. It was during this time when part of a roof fell on me one day, and I broke my ankle. That was why four years of college became five!

I also worked part-time at night doing janitorial work, with two other guys named Jeff Cockrum and Baxter Clark. After hours, when the offices and warehouses would close, we'd go in from about six or seven o'clock and work till midnight.

All of this was part of what I did to make a living. This provided a priceless education in honesty, trust, and *hard work*. After all, my dad had planted these practical seeds in my heart early on in my life.

A solid rock that never rolls

Now, with my graduation in sight, it seemed like a huge relief was within reach. The idea of spreading the Word meant so much more to me than simply being "just another Bible-thumper in the institutional church system." I'd already experienced an incredible transformation since my early days of drugs, depression and delinquency, and now I had radical hope to offer others.

It's always been clear that I wasn't made to fit in. In fact, I believe I was born to stand out. I knew I was never going to fit in doing sermons on Sunday mornings, or wearing a long robe.

With graduation day only weeks ahead of me, I happened upon a rock concert at the Tampa Bay stadium. If I remember right, Alice Cooper was playing. For as long as I could remember, I'd worshipped rock stars like Alice Cooper, Janis Joplin, the Who, Jimmy Hendrix, and the Animals. That was the life I'd been working towards until I met Jesus. Because of this, I held a great awareness and concern about music, and rock/rap culture played an important part in my former destructive lifestyle. Most religious people didn't seem to understand or care about this idolatry like I did.

Barb and I pulled off the road as the crowd was pouring into the stadium. As I looked at her, tears were uncontrollably falling from my eyes. I said, "I have to do something. You go home and don't worry about me. I want to tell all of them about a 'solid rock that never rolls.'"

Although I didn't really have a plan, that was exactly what I did. I stood in the stadium's parking lot wearing a T-shirt, with a Bible in my hand, and as hundreds of people passed by, I would plainly say, "You need Jesus, he's the rock. He's the solid rock. You need to be born-again!"

People walked by me with their jaws on the ground, reacting with, "Oh my God, did you hear what that guy said?"

The *elders* at our church had heard that I was out on the street corner of Dale Mabry Highway, right in the middle of Tampa (at the same stadium where the world-famous Tampa Bay Buccaneers play, even today). I stood on that corner, and spoke directly from my heart. The following Sunday morning, I found myself surrounded by several of these sophisticated church elders, leaders and the beloved Pastor, Dr. Dick Williams from Dallas Theological Seminary.

Understand, I was still a young kid, and I didn't realize how significant these guys were. They literally surrounded me after church and said, "You know, Fred, your intensity, your desire, and the way you reach out to people, we like it, and we want to help you."

Like a dream coming true, they continued, "We'd like to

send you to Moody Bible Institute in Chicago. Don't worry, we'll pay all your expenses to go there. We want you to go through the training for a street-preaching ministry called *Open Air Campaigners.*"

"Aim the loose cannon a little better"

These were the elders at *Christ Community Church*, a well-known and highly-regarded church in Tampa during the 70s. When this group of men (some of who were wealthy and influential - unbeknownst to me at the time) were telling me, "We would like to sponsor you and send you to Chicago for this specialized training," I could hardly believe my ears. I was just a nobody, yet a profound blessing had virtually dropped right in my lap!

"*The Open Air Campaigners* training is designed to teach people to go into the public," the elders told me. "You are gifted in that way, but you need training to help you. You're like a loose cannon, and we'd like you to aim the cannon a little better."

Of course, they were very gracious... and if they hadn't helped me, who knows where I might have ended up.

From Trinity, they sent me to Chicago for an all-summer training, where I was immersed in an in-depth introduction to the organization called *Open Air Campaigners.*

Ravi Zacharias *(left)* **and Fred Kornis** *(right)* **receive their Honorary Doctorates from Trinity College, with president Mark T. O'Farrell** *(center)*

In a flash, I'd hit the ground running in my professional career as a street preacher and communicator. After the six weeks of training was finished, OAC accepted Barb and me as full-time staff, assigning us to their ministry in Baltimore. Baltimore was right next to Washington D.C., and I just laughed, "What's Baltimore?" because I'd never heard of the city before!

What is "faith ministry?"

Now, if you're anything like me, at this point you're probably wondering, "How do we live by faith, what about our finances, and what does it mean to be commissioned into full-time faith ministry?" This was the world I was stepping into.

Basically, there are two different "official" levels to the vocation. You encounter the first level when you initially feel like you want to go into the ministry. Every denomination and church group has an entry level to ministry, and they use different words to describe it. With *Christ Community Church*, I was considered "commissioned," which is like being an apprentice, and it requires the minimum level of qualifications.

Getting commissioned gave me access to the leadership of the local church. This was a significant step, since the local church is the ultimate thing on Earth for God's outreach.

From the start, it was a love-hate thing for me, because local churches are institutions. They are the organizations that I was uncomfortable with, the ones I'd always resisted. Yet despite their quirks, and all the hundreds of denominations and thousands of different little nit-picking doctrinal issues, they're the organization where people go in any given area to learn, worship and fellowship. "Church" may be held in a coffee shop, a barn, in a living room, a bar room, or even under a big shady tree. It could be a small house church, or it may be a big huge mega-church.

Wherever you go, every church has a bureaucracy. They have politics inside the organization, where there are pastors, deacons, elders, and board members. When someone starts moving into ministry, and they have influence in that church, they say that person should be "recognized" in some way (Ephesians 1:7-23).

The *commissioning*, which represents an official recognition by the elders, tells the world that the leaders like what they see. and that there's something about the man or woman that they believe is important to their ministry. They publicly acknowledge that recognition by bringing that person in front to say, "Sally Jones, or Johnny Smith here, is expressing an interest in ministry. We want to bless them in their progress, and we would like to recognize and pray for them."

Later (and it could be after years of hands-on work in the community, or it could be after seminary or college), the church leaders may arrange an *ordination*. That's the big deal. That's when you officially become a Reverend. In the USA, it's also more of a technical, legal position that is recognized by the government. An ordained minister can *marry and bury*, you know, officiating at weddings and funerals.

Since *ordination* is the big one, it's usually the result of a decision by what they call an *ordination council*. Every denomination's process is a little different (Methodists, Presbyterians, Baptists, Lutherans, etc.), but ultimately, that's where you're surrounded by that group of the leaders, and they examine your faith and religious philosophy. It's literally an examination, where they put you under the microscope and ask you personal, psychological and particularly theological questions.

After all, the church leaders want to be sure that you know your theology, and that you're *screwed on the right bolt*. You get examined by this council for several hours, or sometimes even a whole day. You may have to present a paper on theology, but by that time, you've already done all of your in-person "trial periods." The *ordination* is when they "crown you with many crowns." They give you a certificate, and you become "the right reverend holy Joe Blow" or whatever. It is a very serious calling and commitment.

The key point with both formal levels of recognition is that they *set you apart*. This takes you out of the normal group of parishioners, and you're "set apart" for something holy and different for a vocation. In my case, it is to do Christian spiritual work as a Missionary/Evangelist.

Commissioning and *ordination* is a broad umbrella for every denomination. It would cover their teachers, pastors, missionaries, and anybody who is devoted to spiritual Christian work full-time (in whatever official capacity). When someone is *ordained*, they're considered Reverends, Pastors, Clergy, Elders, or whichever title their group uses.

Obviously, it's a long process to get to either of these positions. It's a lot like going through an apprenticeship. Many people spend years helping the church, teaching, counseling, preaching and ministering. All the time, they're learning the influence of Christian ministry.

In the context of my little timeline here, I was commissioned at *Christ Community Church* in 1975. I was officially ordained one year later, in 1976, at *Faith Baptist Church* in Glen Burnie, Maryland.

Throughout school, I was being mentored by George Verwer, Pastors, and all of my college professors. Now I was about to start working full speed ahead with *Open Air Campaigners* in Baltimore, and my new life was about to begin with a bang...literally!

ROGUE MINISTRY

> "I'm sending you out like sheep among wolves. So be as cunning as snakes and as innocent as doves."
>
> *Matthew 10:16*

CHAPTER 5
BREAD, BRAVERY AND BALTIMORE

How wonderful to be a fresh graduate from *Trinity College*, ready for our new ministry.

In June 1976, Barb and I packed up our three kids, a few belongings, and a great big helping of optimism into a U-Haul trailer and moved our family to Baltimore, the city of the Star-Spangled Banner. We already had a connection with David and Elaine Wilson, a precious couple from New Zealand, who were leading the *Open Air Campaigners* office in that city.

We arrived about a month before the country's great bicentennial celebrations were set to begin in Washington D.C. *Open Air Campaigners* had partnered with a couple of other mission groups, and we had official permission to go on the ground beside the Washington monument. We set up a big display, and did all sorts of Biblical presentations for the crowds of people for the 4th of July events, reminding them of our spiritual roots.

Looking out over all the historical buildings, the White

House, the Capitol, etc. was a magnificent view. Of course, Barb and I brought our kids (7-year-old Summer, 5-year-old Jeremy, and 4-year-old Faith) to see the big *Fourth of July* fireworks show, filling the night sky with light, joy and music. What an amazing time to arrive! We were all dressed up in the fashions of 1776 and sharing the timeless Gospel.

We'd never lived in a big city like Baltimore before. One of the first things we noticed was how beautiful and green things looked, as we drove through Virginia, Maryland and other areas we'd passed on our way.

When we arrived in Baltimore, we found a cheap apartment in an area called *The Willows*, and quickly enrolled the kids in Christian school. We didn't have a whole lot of money, but it didn't take long for us to get settled in the community, experiencing the reality of many helpful believers and encouraging local churches.

While I focused on putting my street-preaching skills into action, Barb started getting involved with great people through the *Christian Women's Club*. She soon found that by getting involved in CWC, it was easy to feel at home and build quality relationships. Of all the amazing women involved in CWC, four really stood out: Mary Edna Starner, Jo Knipe, Nancy Cole, and Mary Ellen Iguarta. These women loved and encouraged Barb and our family, and have continued to be part of our lives all these years. They've been perfect examples of God's gift of friendship (Proverbs 17:17).

As for me, the man I went to work with at *Open Air Campaigners* helped me get "on the street" quickly. David Wilson was a former commercial airline pilot from New Zealand, and was a major factor in our decision to choose Baltimore over Chicago. With his soft-spoken, even-tempered manner, I told Barb, "I think I need to go to work with David, so I can mentor under him and receive some of that gentle nature. Maybe I can learn some balance in my intensity."

As I began reaching out among so many people on the streets, I met a kindred spirit in Raleigh Holt. He was the Director of the *Baltimore City Rescue Mission* on the corner of Fourth and Central, where it still operates today. It is a classic mission for the homeless and those in need. At times, you may find two or three hundred men and women eating and sleeping there.

Open Air Campaigners was specializing in all kinds of public street work. We worked in all the neighborhoods, streets, and low-income projects in Baltimore. We had a reputation that people loved, because we were out in the public helping people who never went to church. Most area residents were African-Americans, with such deep, unique "souls." I was envious! I've always believed and said, "I'm white on the outside, but black on the inside!"

Many evenings, Raleigh would have me speak in the *Mission*, because every night before the men would eat, they listened to a Bible message. Right away, I felt closer with the all the guys in the rescue mission than I did with the Sunday morning congregations!

After all, I could speak their language, and they listened carefully to me because I wasn't a religious kind of *Pharisee* talking down to them. I had great success at the *Mission*. Eventually Raleigh gave me and OAC some office space to use.

One day, Raleigh came to me out of the blue and told me he wanted me to do a featured interview. He said, "Your story would be really good for the *Unshackled* radio program."

Unshackled is the longest running radio drama in history, and one of the very few still in production in the USA. The show is aired over 6,500 times weekly around the world, and it's translated in eight languages. It originates at the *Pacific Garden Mission* in Chicago.

The *Baltimore City Rescue Mission* had a dry-out facility for alcoholics, offering food, clothing, and counseling. Being around the place soon taught me the realities of dealing with the men coming in and out off the street.

There was a button beside the door, so when someone on the street wanted something, they'd push the button and a fire alarm bell would go off. It was a loud, unmistakable ringing sound that let us know that someone needed help.

I'll never forget the day when I went downstairs and opened the door to say, "How can we help you?" and saw a guy pressing his face right up to the door. The smell of sweat and booze wafted in, and I soon realized why they didn't let people into the office. Instead, we were instructed to talk to them at the door first.

This guy started cussing me out, yelling, "Give me some *blankety-blank*, I need something else. You guys don't do nothing!" With his other hand, he was urinating on the door…and almost on me!

My first thought was, "You have got to be kidding me!" I discovered that people often acted like animals at the mission. It's the place that fed, clothed, and gave them a bed, but some people were never grateful. God was teaching me a deeper kind of love in those moments!

I had to face the facts that, when you work on the streets doing public street meetings, especially in places like the red-light district and other "not so friendly areas," you're often around people who are crude and tough. They can be mean, and it's often rough work.

That was the real world then and, unfortunately, it's the same way today.

By working in that atmosphere with Raleigh, we became beloved friends. (I was at his bedside before he passed away, many years later.)

Along with the office space, Raleigh also gave me exposure in the community. He invited me to get involved with Jack Beck, his pastor at *North Harford Baptist Church*. Jack and Raleigh decided, "We want Fred to come out and do some special meetings and stir things up." Boy, did they have the right man for that!

I went out to *North Harford* and did special revival meetings at night, Monday through Friday. They invited everyone in the community to come in and hear this Vietnam vet speak. It was a great way to introduce the church to people who normally would not be interested.

One unforgettable night, I was preaching on Hell, outer darkness, and depictions of the damned. I'd described the weeping and wailing, where "the worms never died", and that there's no light at all. Reaching a fever pitch, I sincerely stormed, "Really, do you believe in this? I mean, is this really that important?" (Luke 16:19-31).

All of a sudden, Pastor Beck, who was seated in the pews with the rest of the congregation, let out a howling scream that stood the hairs up on the back of everyone's neck!

Everyone in the room was petrified, but the Pastor couldn't control himself. My sermon had lit up his imagination, triggering his emotions about Hell, and he cried out.

After everybody kind of gulped, I continued on, but I'll never forget how my words had stirred the pastor so completely that the image came alive for him, personally. Especially since he had spent his whole life studying and teaching the Scriptures, it was like a revelation. It seemed like he'd just heard the Scripture passage for the first time in his life. That was when it became real for him (and everyone around him, too).

Cultivating the seeds of worldwide ministry

As I grew and became more and more involved in the cities, a quote I'd once read continued to haunt my life:

"As long as there are millions who have never heard the good news or had an opportunity to have a Bible... it will be impossible for me to give all my time, energy and resources to the people who already have both."

As an *Open Air Campaigner*, I was usually out on the streets in Baltimore and Washington, D.C. We'd also visit Ocean City, Atlantic City, New York City, Boston, and other places for outreaches.

Remember, we were street preachers. We would go out in the public, and do meetings and programs just about anywhere. This could be at the beach, in the parks, at bus stops, subways, neighborhoods, the projects – anywhere God led. We especially liked to do creative programs with children in the tougher neighborhoods.

I still had an underlying, haunting guilt that I was pouring out my life in a city, a culture and a country that seemingly was overdosed with Christian information. There are churches on almost every street corner, and all kinds of religious opportunities. You could tune in on television, the radio, even computers, to listen to the gospel. You could also buy Bibles in any bookstore. It's all here, and easily accessible.

I was realizing more and more that we live with such riches, even in regards to our opportunities and freedoms in North America.

Don't get me wrong, I've always been very thankful that we have so much, and that we are probably one of the most blessed cultures in world history. We have so many things, choices and possibilities to access information, it's nearly unbelievable.

But when you go to a place like India and you get off the plane, it's like you have just stepped back 1,000 years, especially in the remote villages.

One *billion* people live in India. That is almost four times the number of people in America! Plus, the population of India today continues to increase by over a million every month!

Many live in very primitive conditions - physically, financially, and intellectually. They don't have many opportunities, and the majority have never heard of Jesus. If you would go into an average village and say, "Hey, you know about Jesus?" they may look you straight in the eye and say, "He doesn't live here. He may be down the road, somewhere else."

The saddest of all, though, is that they're clueless and hopeless for any opportunity to know about Christianity. The images of all of this in my mind were starting to overtake every waking hour for me. As this awareness went deeper into my heart and my thoughts, I realized I had to be careful about how I talked with people about my vision and my changing priorities. "I'm walking on thin ice now," I'd tell myself, "because once I become a threat to all of the focus on this culture, then they'll really withdraw from me."

Putting down some roots

Meanwhile, after three years in *The Willows* apartments, we were able to buy an old house for our growing family. We'd just had our fourth child, Vanessa, and definitely needed more space.

The house was a Godsend. It was one of the original homes in the area. Our realtor stated that some potential buyers had been concerned because it had been sitting empty for over five years. It was partially boarded up, but Barb and I fell in love with it. We loved the 10-foot ceilings, the pocket doors, and its welcoming wrap-around front porch.

Somehow, we borrowed the money to buy the house for $35,000. It was complete with wood floors, six bedrooms, and a large back yard, which would come in handy as the children grew. At last, itlooked like we'd decided to put down some roots on Hollins Ferry Road in Baltimore.

A classic Fred Kornis sermon we'll never forget

Moving just as quickly as our home life, my life as a street preacher with OAC was teaching me to use my intense energy for good. Sometimes it worked out that way, and sometimes, well, not so much.

As I met people "in their world" on the streets every day, I'd constantly remind myself of my little prayer under the stairway at college. I never wanted to be thought of as one of those "professionals" I'd seen in the religious organizations or on TV. I've always been a street guy, and wanted to stay that way.

Both you and I know that if you talk to 10 people on the street in Baltimore, Toronto or New York City, many would say, "All the church wants is your money." But that's not true. In my case, and with the teams of well-meaning street preachers and missionaries I've worked with, it's not about money at all.

With that thought always in the back of my mind, my true feelings came out in a sermon I gave at the *Overlea Baptist Church*. It was a classic old stone building on the North side of Baltimore that looked like something out of the English countryside.

Since I was the new "guest preacher" standing up in front of the congregation, I was eager to clear the slate right off the bat, and I let them know where I was coming from. Whenever I spoke to any new group, they all seemed to have their guard up at first. They were probably thinking, "Okay, what's this guy up to? He probably wants our money."

In order to counter that thought, I went to this weird extreme, declaring in my loud, passionate voice, "Listen, I don't want your stinking money! You can take your money and eat it. I want you to give your life to the Lord.

That's all I want."

Well, when you say that in the average congregation, they are shocked. It's like dropping a bomb. Of course, I really stirred up a hornet's nest with the *scribes and Pharisees* of that church, to think that I'd come across so critical.

Needless to say, I wasn't invited back to speak at that church the following week. We all knew my heart was in the right place, but as soon as the words left my mouth, I knew I needed to come up with a better way of communicating my sentiments!

As it turned out, when I was back at that same church two or three years later, I came to find out I had made quite an impression on one of the parishioners in particular. A blessed little old lady, who I'd guess was close to 80 years of age, came up to me and said, "Do you remember when you were here last time? You screamed and said you didn't want our money."

I admit, I was humbled by this point, and I'm sure it showed on my face, as I smiled sheepishly at the old woman who was wagging her finger at me as she spoke.

She continued, "You know," she said, "I had a check already written out for you, before you stood up to speak. When you said that, I tore it up." Once again, I ate a piece of humble pie, and I begged her for forgiveness. Thank the Lord, she was gracious to this young zealot.

God's still working on me today, teaching me to

communicate my passion more effectively.

Breaking into the routine of mission work

Preaching and mission work had become my standard routine. After months of long, but rewarding days, I began to sense the impression that many people had become critical of what the work was like. I discovered that some people can be much harder on you if you're in the ministry, than if you're in a "normal" job that makes you travel. It often feels like you are in a fish bowl, being watched by everyone around you.

Fred doing street meetings in Washington... and everywhere!

For example, Barb would hear well-meaning friends and acquaintances say, "Well, it's not right that he's dumping all the responsibility on you for raising the family." Barb would tell me it's like Job, who had three friends who were just more of a downer than anything. "People come to encourage you or support you," she'd say, "but instead of helping you, they're tearing us down, because we live differently than they do."

The purpose of missions is to help unreached people. It takes a special person with the kind of heart to see, understand, and appreciate what these servants of the Lord are going through. Praise the Lord for all the encouragers God brings into our lives, to give us love and support at just the right time.

Sometimes people only see the negative, thinking you're trying to get out of doing something. I'd hear people say, "You just don't want to be disciplining your children," or "You want to run away from family life, so you go overseas." Such critical words hurt deeply, but we have always put our trust in God, and that He's called us to this work as our purpose.

"Well, that's where the money is!"

I remember one guy in particular, who asked us what it was like living as missionaries. After telling him how it could be challenging, but the rewards were worth it, Barb asked him, "Why do you ask?"

His reply nearly floored us, when he said, "Well, that's where the money is!"

Barb and I looked at him and said, "Are you kidding me?" Here we were trying to make ends meet for our family of six, living on only $1200 a month, or whatever happened to come in from donations that particular month.

Maybe that doesn't sound bad for the early 70's, but we were sending our kids to Christian school, which alone cost us $310 every month. That meant we were actually living on less than $900, which had to cover everything including rent, utilities, car, food, clothes, etc.

That was why we looked at him in disbelief, going, "That's where the money is? Really?"

Unfortunately, it seems people can have a lot of misconceptions about ministry and mission work. For example, many believe that ministers only work one day a week, for a few hours on Sunday. LOL!

They don't think twice about the minister who goes to visit people at the hospital at all hours of the day, or the one who spends hours and hours studying and preparing for a weekly sermon. Providing individual and family counseling, doing weddings and funerals, and so much more, often go unnoticed as well.

In our case, there has never been a "salary" paid by any church or organization. We have only received what was donated for us, which is unpredictable. There's also no pension or retirement funds awaiting us when we turn 65. (Oh? We are already 68!)

No matter how many times we try to explain this to people, most will never fully understand the time involved, or the reality of being a faith-based missionary.

We truly have to rely on God, and trust Him to provide for us. Even a kind gift of $10 lets us know they understand.

There's often a big difference between people's perception and this reality. I guess it's like they say, "There's always three truths... their truth, your truth, and the real truth."

I wonder how the Apostle Paul was "paid" for his work? (2 Corinthians 11:21-33).

The sketch board specialist

Fortunately, progress was happening day by day. As I learned more *Open Air* methods over the years, I became a specialist at communicating using a sketch board and object lessons in public places, churches, camps, and anywhere we had opportunities.

Our presentations were great attention-getters, and we'd gather small crowds of people everywhere we went. People would pack in around my sketch board as I'd create captivating sketches, drawing words and pictures on my sketch board. I spoke as I painted, and I would raise questions like, "Hey, do you believe God exists?"

Sure, we'd get some hecklers, but it was always out in the open, and we had trained teams with us. The team stood in the crowd and helped get the crowd involved. Then we would all provide counseling, prayer, and literature for anyone who showed interest.

We would go out day and night, looking for places to share our teachings. We even created black-light sketches, which we did on the beaches of the Jersey Shore.

The best part about *Open Air Campaigners* is that they're all about reaching people outside the institutions. OAC was particularly focused on public places, beaches, parks, ghettos, etc. It was all based on the model of how Jesus communicated – on the streets, out in the public.

If you did a word study of the New Testament, you'd find that Jesus spoke about 80% of the time in a public place - on a street, a hillside, or outside with the fishermen. Very rarely would you find Him speaking inside an institution.

However, I was becoming more and more aware that the "church" was becoming private instead of public.

One afternoon in D.C., one of my team members told me that he saw Henry Kissinger walk by and look right at us. Overall, we weren't really aware of who was watching or listening, so I think we'll all be surprised when we get to Heaven and find out. "His Word will not return void" (Isaiah 55:11).

A threat to challenge our shared existence?

I couldn't resist thinking that my success in reaching *the unreachables* out on the streets was becoming a thorn in the sides of some institutional religious leaders (the *scribes and Pharisees*, as I jokingly referred to them).

I'd begun to develop a lingering mistrust of church leaders who seemed to be afraid, insecure, and would hide in their congregations (Matthew 23:1-39). I felt I was reaching people they weren't getting to, and I was doing it in a way they wouldn't. So I'd settled into feeling like I was "rejected and shunned" by them.

The problem with that way of thinking is, there isn't a right or wrong way of reaching people. I had condemned them, thinking, "Well this bunch of so-and-so's, they have no business standing behind that pulpit, hiding. Why don't they get out in the public, if they believe what they're saying?"

However, while I was condemning toward them, they were also condemning toward me, saying, "Oh, look at him." It's sad, but when your ego gets ahold of you, it's hard to have unity. We have to remember, we are all different of parts and members of the same "body" (1 Corinthians 12:1-31).

After learning the hard way over the last 40 years, I now realize that everything has its place. Yes, there's a place for all those choirs to stand and sing. Yes, there are also the places where Jesus went out, and He dealt with the stinky fishermen!

The Highway to Hell, right there in Baltimore!

Another large Christian organization called *Word of Life* (a well-known and worldwide inter-denominational school and ministry based in upper New York) had sent a team of students down to work with me. They needed to get experience working in the city and in public places.

We happened to be out one day in South Baltimore, which was known as being a pretty tough area of the city. We could feel the tension in the air as we set up in front of the high school. At the edge of the sidewalk, a car was waiting to pick up the driver's friends. The car's windows were down, and the music was blaring so loud you could probably hear it a mile away.

The song that was blasting from the radio was called, "Highway to Hell," a chart-topper by the hard-rock group AC/DC.

Remember, I'm an ex-druggie rock-and-roller, and this music was in my DNA. All of a sudden, with the song blasting away across from us, I started drawing quickly on my sketch-board. As I painted, the kids were attracted to watch and listen.

In a flash of inspiration, I started writing my bold title "The Highway to Heaven" on top, all while the AC/DC song was playing in the background.

The next thing you know, I'm painting a cross and drawing Jesus saying, "I am the way, the truth, and the life." Well, right in the middle of that moment, with probably 20 or 30 kids standing around the sidewalk, a security guard comes out and very rudely confronts me, saying, "You have to stop this right now, and get out of here."

I looked him in the eye and said, as I had so many other times in public places, "Wait a minute, this is a public sidewalk. I can do this, if I'm not hurting anybody or any business.

"Remember the First Amendment in the Constitution?!"

Keep in mind, I'm near the end of my story and the music in the background is still blaring. The group of missionary students were huddled around with the regular students, while this dynamic moment was going on. I would have wrapped it up gracefully in a couple of minutes anyway, but this man, full of hate and aggression, would not stop.

"That's it, you're under arrest!"

The security guard kept forcefully trying to get me to leave, and at one point he even reached over to grab my paintbrush and my paint-board. It made no difference to him that I was almost finished. I was so aware of those needy kids watching, open to receive God's love. "Hey, you can't do this!" I pleaded.

The next thing I knew, he'd put me in handcuffs in front of everyone! He proceeded to take me inside the school, and called the police. When the police came, they arrested me and put me in a police paddy wagon, right beside two other prisoners who'd been picked up for forging checks.

It was like a scene right out of the movies. While we rode in the paddy wagon, I was handcuffed to one seat, and the other guys were handcuffed to the seats across from me. As I watched, the two of them were taking the checks that they'd been writing, and frantically tore them up into little pieces before we made it to the police station.

I hope you never get to discover what getting arrested is like in real life. Once you get into the criminal system, you become a nobody, and they don't care who you are.

The people who transport you are not the same people who process you at the jailhouse, so they had no idea where I'd come from, or for what reason. To be honest, it left me feeling hopeless, as I was thrown into the system.
After they kept me in jail overnight, I was given a hearing for the next month and then released. But I guess word had spread like wildfire around the city, because there were about 20 pastors who showed up at the jailhouse. They were in an outrage that I had been stopped on a public street like that, and because I was now being charged with trespassing and disturbing the peace. I was only trying to share the GOOD NEWS!?

Unexpectedly, as I entered the packed court room the next month, I witnessed a miracle happen right before my eyes. The judge read the charge aloud, looked up at me and threw it out!

He said, "This is not even a case worthy of my time." You should have heard it, the place exploded in applause, with all these pastors grateful for freedom of speech.

"I have some good news and some bad news"

Barb told me that she'd found out about my incarceration when she'd gotten a call from Tom Major, one of my co-workers. He said, "Barb, I have some good news and some bad news. What do you want first?"
"The bad news," Barb told him.

Tom replied, "Fred got arrested."

With her sense of humor poking through her fears, she asked him, "Well, what's the good news?"

Tom shot back, "Nobody else was." Then he continued, "I didn't know how to tell you."

Barb was thinking, "Okay, good news and bad news, so what do we do now?"

Barb decided to call our pastor for advice and direction. He told her to call *Heritage Foundation*, a Christian organization that sets you up with lawyers and legal assistance.

As it turned out, everything worked out fine, and I can laugh about it now. I still smile thinking about it to this day, saying to myself, "Of all the times I should have been arrested as a kid, this is what you get me for? Something good and not wrong?"

Yes, God works in mysterious ways.

> "They won the victory over Satan because of the blood of the Lamb and the word of their testimony. They didn't love their life so much that they refuse to give it up."
>
> *Revelation 12:11*

CHAPTER 6
BLOOD IN INDIA

As we continued to build momentum and influence for Christ on the streets, David Wilson and I were connected with many churches, schools and Bible colleges throughout Maryland and the East Coast. Often, a component of their school curriculum required the students to get actual Christian service outreach experience in the field.

We were in charge of taking groups of students for public outreach at least once a week, probably a total of 20-30 times throughout the year.

We were grateful for the extra help the students could bring, and they were thrilled to see the effects of live street-preaching in action. This would also deepen their awareness and focus, to reach out to the UN-churched world.

"Well, I never let it go"

One week, a bright-eyed undergrad named Vicky Rogers showed up with a group from *Washington Bible College*. She had chosen to join our open-air street meetings, and was ready to connect with people in the projects around Washington DC.

One day, we'd found a location where children were playing and decided to stop and do our program. We unload the OAC van, set up our sketch boards, and started singing and telling Bible stories. The best part about our presentations was keeping the audiences engaged with fun interaction and drama.

The stories changed, but the mission was always the same – to spread the Word. As people gathered, the college students would stand or sit among the children, parents, and others who were listening.

When each of our sketch-board programs was done, the college students and volunteers asked the audience questions. ,Some counseled and prayed with people who were interested, and others helped with equipment and literature.

With everything packed up at the end of that day, Vicky sat in one of the van's middle seats for the drive back to the college. She sang along happily with the group, as the van crawled along in the bumper-to-bumper rush-hour traffic.

As usual, Vicky was carrying her small New Testament. She tapped her finger on the cover to the beat of the music as they sang. Suddenly, her eyes widened, and her heart skipped a beat when she saw that the car in front of them had completely stopped moving.

The driver quickly swerved to miss it, but the van was top heavy, and it rolled over onto its side in the middle of the street. I was shocked to see this happen in front of me, as I followed close behind them in another vehicle. With oncoming traffic merging into the lanes around us to give us space, I jumped out and onto the top of the overturned vehicle, and started pounding on the door to get it open. I kept praying that no one had been hurt, and the gasoline would not blow up!

Seconds seemed to tick by like hours, but I made it to the side door, opened it, and started reaching my arm down to hoist the startled students out one by one. Vicky grabbed my hand to pull herself up, looked me straight in the eye, and said, "We never know how much time we have left on this Earth."

Fortunately, there were no serious injuries, only one boy's jammed finger and Vicky's pinky sprain. When she noticed her pain at the scene of the accident, one of her friends had unwrapped Vicky's scarf from her neck and tied it around her finger... using Vicky's Bible as a splint! I'll never forget how the ER doctor chuckled as he looked at Vicky's finger and said, "We've never seen a splint like that before."

"Well, I never let it go," she replied simply, referring to her New Testament text.

I didn't realize it at the time, but the life-and-death sense of urgency the accident highlighted in Vicky's consciousness that day, would bond her to faithful mission service for the rest of her life. She became both a valued colleague and a close friend in the years to come.

A whole different world

Still working from our office at the *Baltimore City Rescue Mission*, I was constantly talking and praying with David Wilson, OAC's director in the city. We would frequently discuss theology and our philosophies, along with the day-to-day challenges, strategies and triumphs of our street ministry. The reality of India, and the unreached masses in poor developing countries, was a growing concern in both of our hearts.

In 1979, David Wilson went to India for a year, and I became OAC's Acting-Director for Baltimore. During this time, God kept connecting me with more believers and churches who shared my passion and loved my heart for reaching the unreached of the world. Thank God for those who encouraged us, you know who you are.

I went to the Indian Embassy in D.C. and formally applied for visas for our whole family, but we were denied. It turns out that Barb had actually been praying secretly for God to shut that door! She was happy and supportive for me to go to India, but not the whole family. As a result, we eventually learned how much more could be accomplished, with less money and fewer complications, when we didn't bring the entire family to a strange place.

Still, the more I thought of and prayed about India, the more I was convinced I needed to go there and share whatever "crumbs" I could. In 1982, I received a special invitation to travel to the country, for a short-term mission/training trip for local leaders. I took a temporary leave from my assignment at OAC, and made plans to meet Ray Eicher and his OM team in Bombay. Barb was always supportive, and knew the great vision in my heart. She even gave me the $1500 we had in savings to pay for the trip!

After a grueling, sleepless 24-hour flight, I stepped off the plane at 2am and tried to adjust to the pungent wave of smells that greeted my nostrils. Standing among the eerie sounds, sights and shocking atmosphere of this new environment,. I was all alone... with only $40 dollars in cash on me. I made my way to an old British "Ambassador" taxi outside the airport.

Unfortunately, I was unable to communicate with the driver, which caused us to spend an hour weaving through the dark dreary streets of the massive city. Thousands of "bodies" lay on the sidewalks, where so many people actually lived. I found my way to a tiny community inside Bombay (now Mumbai) called *Nana Chowk*.

It wasn't long before I discovered a culture and a set of beliefs that were totally different from what I knew at home.

Who's untouchable?

For generations, all of Hinduism was laced with what we know of in the west as blatant discrimination. Although the issues were similar to those the US experienced with slaves several generations ago, India's social structure is much worse. This social structure, known as the *caste system*, has been followed in India for thousands of years.

As a result of this unofficial, but silently-enforced class structure, the Dalit were normally known and treated as "untouchables." Yet this group of people makes up one-fourth of the billion people in India.

It shocked me to see how most people blew this situation off as normal, and even tried to justify it. Actually, I learned that this very dark *caste system* meant almost 300 million people (more than the entire population of the United States at the time) were left with barely any legal status, or even any recognition as citizens. They were virtually on the brink of being considered even less than slaves in their own country. On top of this, it was "illegal" for them to become Christians.

Much like the homeless I'd seen in Baltimore and Kansas City, everyone knew the *untouchables* were around, but nobody really wanted to deal with them. I don't think many of the Dalit even had anything like birth certificates, civil rights or freedoms like others in their country.

In addition, and most mind-boggling to me, their *untouchable* status meant that they couldn't even choose their own religion. Their only option was being forced to follow Hinduism.

The trickle-down effect, right down to today, is that many of the Dalit are illiterate. They don't know anything about this stuff, and life goes on for them from day to day. Many are like squatters, and believe this is their only fate for life. That's why I was there to offer them another choice.

My heart, and my involvement with India, were instantly drawn together like a magnet because of these people. There's incredible need everywhere, but often, it seems that what you hear in the news, and what is real life, are not nearly the same thing. I still wonder where all the protestors and human rights activists are concerning India!?

Enter the fighter's instinct

I was instinctively triggered to remember the time I was chased home by bullies, as a fifth-grader in Kansas. I remembered how my father, a member of the Golden Gloves movement in the US during the 1940s, was a champion boxer and a tough, physical man. He fought like a tiger when he was young, and when I was born, he immediately started pouring this fighter's instinct into me. He would push me and push me to the edge, often to the point of tears and beyond. But he made sure I learned how to box, how to position my feet, and ultimately how to retain my dignity.

As he was teaching me how to dodge and move and keep my guard, even as a little child, the boxing instinct really settled deep into me. This evolved into some serious, bloody fist-fighting.

When bullies chased me home from school one day, my dad saw it all. He was at the door as I tried to escape into the house. When he saw my attackers outside, yelling and taunting, he looked at me and said, "It's either me or them, you take your choice. Because I'm either gonna knock the hell outta you, or they are. You better get out there and take care of them."

That's how I learned to fight for my life.

I went outside swinging and hitting, bashing and kicking the bullies who had chased me until they took off and left me alone. I think it taught me the courage to survive, and gave me a special intolerance for bullying of any kind. I also think it made me even more confident and aggressive.

It's in my heartbeat

Now this is where I'm afraid... I mean, I'm sensitized that you and I are probably seeing the world through a different lens. It may be, either it doesn't make sense or you flat-out disagree. Either way, just stick with me here.

When I talk about people who haven't even had the opportunity to consider their rights, religion, or spiritual choices in other countries, I want to help them. They are not overflowing in riches and opportunities, like we are in the Western world. What choices do these 2000-year old systems offer to guide people through their daily life with faith, hope and love - now and forever?

Only Jesus offers it all... freely!

After all my experience from the beginning - including my childhood, my conversion, my training and the people I've connected with throughout the world - I've had this growing, constant, and deep conviction.

Think of that word. A *conviction* is something you'd die for.

There are countless orphans... among 1 BILLION people

I would die for this cause. I have risked my life over and over, because I believe this is the ultimate reality.

I believe in absolutes.

Now, this is where the secular humanist will scream and pull their hair out. This is where they're going to hit us over the head with, "There are no absolutes. The only thing that's absolute is that there are no absolutes." But I believe that statement is absurd.

I don't allow that nonsense. I don't believe them for a

second, because I believe there are absolutes!

Whether you're having brain surgery or jumping out of an airplane with a parachute, unless you believe in some kind of absolutes, you're going to die. If you don't stop at the red lights in busy intersections, you're going to die. If you drink poison, you're going to die.

Now, let me bring that back to the question about whether it's Buddhism, Hinduism, Muslim, Paganist, or secularist in general. I believe they are sincerely wrong. Being sincere does not make anything right or true. Everyone is not right.

I'm a Bible believer. I have embraced the Judeo-Christian Scriptures and it's in my blood and heartbeat that one God created the heavens and the Earth. Jesus was crucified because He believed that.

I believe there is one God who actually exists. He's not up for grabs, like you can just write any name on it that you want - whether that be an elephant, monkey, dog or a monk. He is a distinct, jealous God. Just read through Scriptures like Isaiah 40-45, Deuteronomy 4:24, and 1 Timothy 2:5 and you'll see.

The history of Judaism and Islam is real because they all came from Abraham. The Muslims came out of his line and it's all Biblical. It's all in the Old Testament (Genesis 16-22).

If you look deeper into this, you can trace it all back to

Adam and Eve, Noah, Moses, Abraham and even up to Jesus. These are not cartoon characters made up like Donald Duck or Mickey Mouse. These are absolute historical figures that, like them or not, are as real as Winston Churchill or Donald Trump. They were literal people in a literal time and place (Matthew 1:1-17).

One time when I was in a village in India, I put my camera down on a big volcanic-looking rock to take a picture of the sunset, and some guy came running toward me. He was talking rapidly in his native language, and he looked terrified. My translator told me, "Stop that!"

I looked around and asked, "What's the problem?"

He said, "You just put your camera on top of his god."

Do I believe that guy needed to know a little more about life, education or choices? Yes.

To put it another way, let's use a popular phrase you may have heard, but say it in an entirely different context. We often think of Pro-choice in regards to abortion, but have you ever considered it in respect to having a choice about anything – including religion?

When it comes to faith, education, or life in general, do you believe in being Pro-choice?

In this situation, I'm so pro-choice, I make the pro-choicers look liberal! I'm fanatically pro-choice. I believe Muslims need a choice. I believe Hindus, Buddhists, atheists and Paganists all need a choice.

The Bible says, "For God so loved the world, that He gave His only begotten Son, that *whosoever* believes in Him, will never perish, but have eternal life" (John 3:16). I think every single person needs a choice, so I present people with a choice in a kind, thoughtful, and loving way.

Throughout India, I've laid on floors with rats crawling near us. I've tried to sleep where ten of us were laying on the floor, and along the edge of the wall, giant rats were watching us, waiting for something they could eat.

Did you know you can't kill them, though?

You can't do anything to these rats, because many of the Indian gods have rats and mice involved with worship. On the bottom of statues of Ganesha (an elephant headed Hindu god), temples always have mice and rats. They have hundreds, even thousands of these temples all over the country. Hindus believe this god is "transported" on the back of a rat. The far-reaching implications are practical, and scary.

India has gods of many kinds. Some examples include gods of monkeys, gods of the elephants, gods of the eyeball, gods of babies, etc. They are all different gods, but often on the bottom of each of their monuments, there will be carvings of little rats and mice. In a small town called Deshnoke, between New Delhi and the western border of India, there is another temple for rats.

The superstitions teach that 600 years ago, people were reincarnated into rats.

Knowing this explains a lot about my experience with the rock, and the man who thought it was a god.

This kind of theology goes back thousands of years, and has been handed down through generations.

Their view of gods is bloody, and I have personally witnessed live animal sacrifices where I became physically sick. The goddess Kali is known as a blood thirsty god, where humans have been sacrificed in the past. A blood sacrifice is a serious act to appease the gods. Similar things are seen around the world with many religions.

I know you may have chuckled at the thought of monkey gods and holy reincarnated rats that carry gods on their backs, but when you laugh, I weep. I have been there. I have spent almost 40 years pouring my life out for India. I almost died there. My blood was left on the roadside in a near-fatal accident in Bihar. I love India!

I don't think it's right to see people giving their lives and their devotion to a rat. I think they do need another choice, and the God of the Bible is not a God who needs a rat to travel. *Blood* is truly at the heart of the Bible. All the animal or human blood ever sacrificed to appease and pay for sin is only a dim shadow, pointing to the only final and ultimate sacrifice of the perfect Lamb of God, Jesus! *(Read Hebrews 9 for this glorious fact)*

The option is, it's not forced, but it's like, "Would you like to hear about this God of the Bible, the one who created the heavens and the Earth? The one who made the rocks and the stars... *and* the rats? The sun can't be a god, because this God made the sun. The God who loves you so much that He came to earth to die for you on the cross, rise from the dead, and will return to take those who believe in Him to Heaven forever. Now that is a choice to think about!" That fact is called the GOOD NEWS!!

With many in India, the poverty and sickness often cuts their life span short. The Bible offers a whole new way of life (John 10:10). Even the western Christian influence that you and I have enjoyed, whether we accept it or not, has come from a Judeo-Christian theology that is factual, and it has helped us in endless and practical ways.

I know the government and our western society is not perfect. I would never say it is, but the quality of the Judeo-Christian theology has built our culture.

Lately, I think we're moving towards losing it, though. I think we will, if we go off and worship the rocks in our backyard, and revere the rats as our reincarnated family members.

The problem now, and why I live with constant rejection, is because many in my culture (some family, some friends, and many of my peers) don't like anything to be absolute. "We have to keep it nice and gray," they say, "that's called tolerance."

Billy Graham figured it out long ago, saying, "The problem in our world today is that tolerance has become God."

I say, "Politically correct crap drives me crazy."

All roads don't lead to Dallas, and all roads don't lead to Heaven!

A theological can of worms

I mentioned a while ago about those two words "go" and "all" - two tiny hinges that swing the big doors in life. This concept is so deep, and so serious. If you take the word *go*, and then you take the word *all*, they are big, big concepts. I could go on for an hour right now about the concept of communication. My whole life is about communication.

After all, Jesus was a Communicator. God is a great Communicator. In the very first chapter of Genesis, it says over and over, "God said," "He Said," "God spoke."

Twenty-six times, over and over, it tells of God speaking. That's how the whole origin of life appears; it comes out of God speaking. Then Jesus spoke, and he inspired the disciples who followed him, who then told people, "Never a man spoke like that man." (John 7:46)

The entire New Testament, and all of life, is a reflection and a result of communication.

That's the opposite of being selfish. If you're generous

128

and you're selfless, you will share. You will give. You will speak. The ideas, thoughts and communication you share gives influence and hope. It gives meaning, purpose, and choices. Reality is serious business.

That's why I have been on a fanatical trip of communication for the last 40 years. That is also why I use books, Bibles, my voice, sketch-boards, flipcharts, object lessons, gospel illustrations, etc. It's all about getting people's attention and communicating another choice.

That is all my life has been - training others and doing the work myself. I am especially drawn to go "where the fields are white unto harvest" (Matthew 9:35-38), where people can only wonder, "Is there more to life??"

I say there is. It's Jesus. He said, "Don't cast your pearls before the pigs." In other words, don't waste your pearls on people who don't even recognize or appreciate the value or the wisdom... or who don't even care about the choice you are offering them.

A long time ago, when I started going to third-world countries like Mexico, India and the Philippines, I realized that there are groups of people in the world who are open and hungry. There are people who are appreciative, thankful, teachable and ready for truth.

As I've looked at the USA, Canada, and many of the western countries, I see the multi-billion-dollar religious systems that throw their money at their little entertainment thing on Sunday morning over and over every week. The *fanatics* who intensely worship celebrities, superstars, and earthly pleasures definitely worship the wrong god (Romans 1).

This makes me want to puke. "I'm going to *go* into *all* the world!" (Matthew 28). I'm going to share the gospel with every creature. The people who are the least, they're the ones I call the greatest opportunity (Romans 15:20-21).

In other words, "Why do we keep feeding people on the front row over and over, when the people on the back row are starving to death?"

As soon as I'd experienced India in 1982, I knew I'd be back. I not only made it back there, but I've been there just about every year since then. I've poured my heart and hundreds of thousands of dollars into India. I've invested into thousands of people by educating, training, buying vehicles, helping build and operate orphanages, constructing church buildings and homes, and giving out books and Bibles. India is one of the places that has the least amount of Christian information or opportunity, and is right in the middle of the 10-40 window.

They needed it, they wanted it, they were hungry for it!

When you go into a Hindu village, or often even a Muslim village, you see how they are so innocent and open! If I go down the street here in the US, which I do at times, I often get mocked, laughed at, or even cussed out. A perfect example of this actually happened a few weeks ago. I was standing outside of a bus stop in downtown Kansas City doing my little rope trick, presenting God's good news to about 20 people. Many listened to me and even took my booklet, but there were two or three of them who mocked me and walked off.

They would rarely reject us in a simple Indian village.

There's a new Kornis in town!

Back in the USA after my first trip to India, I jumped back into OAC and street-preaching with an unquenchable fire inside me.

In late 1979, Barb and I welcomed our fourth child into the world. Miraculously, our daughter Vanessa was born on the same day as her 7-year-old sister, Faith. Vanessa was named after our precious African-American friend, Vanessa Carter.

When Faith realized our new baby had the same birthday as her, she snapped out of being babyish herself, and said, "She's mine. She was born on my birthday. You other two get out of the way, because she's my gift."

Months earlier, when our eight-year-old son Jeremy first learned that we were going to have another baby, he went up to his mom and said, "It's not fair. It's just not fair. You have Daddy to sleep with. Summer has Faith. I don't have anybody. Can you buy me a teddy bear?"

Barb soothed his feelings by telling him, "Oh, honey, I think I have something better. Mommy's having a baby.

Maybe Jesus is going to give you a baby brother."

Looking back, she never should have said that to him, because for months, he'd convinced himself he was getting a baby brother. When he got on the phone to his mom after she gave birth at the hospital, the first thing Jeremy said was, "Did I get my baby brother?"

Barb told him, "Oh, honey, I'm sorry, you have a baby sister." Jeremy said that he already had two, he didn't want another one… and he hung up the phone!

He didn't talk to Barb again for almost two weeks. He was like, "You lied to me." It was almost funny, but we learned never to say things like that again!

Of course, Jeremy eventually started talking to all of us again. In fact, up until the time Vanessa turned four, all her siblings used to fight over who was going to have her sleep with them. They were all very close, then and now.

Broadening my reach with OAC and beyond

Every day we continued to go into the streets and public places to share the Word.

I had heard of Ralph Winter, a man in Pasadena, California, who'd created a movement targeting *the 10/40 window.* through an organization called the U.S. Center for World Missions. This *10/40 window* region is claimed to have the highest number of unreached people in the world, and has the least access to the Christian message and resources. (The U.S. Center for World Missions recently changed their name to *Frontier Ventures*).

Barb and I invested financially in the U.S. Center for World Missions, and started following that movement as soon as we'd found out that it was all about connecting with hidden, unreached people. (Recently, I have also had the privilege of promoting and helping to teach their *"Perspectives"* course.)

My relationships were increasing, with me preaching in churches in and around Baltimore, working basically in the streets, rescue missions and jails. I became an official chaplain in Baltimore City jail, and in the city hospital. Plus, I was taking teams of college students out twice a week, to give them a taste of public street work.

Meanwhile, my "side interest" in India kept growing, taking its place closer to the forefront of my mind.

As the pace continued to pick up like this, something had to give… or maybe I should say "someone" had to give. When they did, the next chapter in my life took an unexpected, but rewarding twist!

> "Honor the Lord with your wealth and with the first and best part of all your income. Then your Barns will be full, and your vats will overflow with fresh wine."
>
> *King Solomon, Proverbs 3:9-10*

CHAPTER 7
FIERCE POVERTY, IRREPRESSIBLE SPIRIT

A new decade was opening before us, and I was fortunate to get involved with several opportunities for travel to India and the Philippines with my OAC colleague, Barry Tetley, from 1980 to 1983. (Barry is the author of the unique Sowers Program.)

I learned the powerful importance of *the seed* (Luke 4:8-15) as our work continued. It seemed that the effects of our ministry were so greatly magnified there.

The seed

For example, I remember giving a simple $25 check to a man named Lawrence. Lawrence lived in the Bihar-Jharkhand area on the border of Nepal and Bangladesh, that had a population of over 135 million people. This small donation enabled him to buy a parcel of land as a home for his new family. Within a few years, we had helped him build a house for his three sons, and he also created a multipurpose center on the compound for his local community and ministry.

With my passion for global ministry growing deeper with each passing month, I was frustrated when the Indian

Embassy in Washington refused my requests to move my entire family to India. I think it was denied because they suspected that we were some kind of missionary people.

Barb told me later that she was actually so thrilled when we were turned down. She had been praying that God would shut that door, because she didn't really want to go to India.

I continued to look at alternatives to be in developing nations outside of the USA. When I noticed that the only country in Asia that spoke English was the Philippines, I figured it would be easier for a foreigner to set up shop and "hit the ground running" in that tropical country. It was also definitely more family-friendly than India.

Within weeks, the answer to my prayers appeared when I received a formal invitation from another OAC colleague, Barry Tetley.

Barry and I had worked together doing a training program in India back in 1982, so when he offered me a position to come to the Philippines and help him do seminars, I jumped at the chance. I requested to be released from my duties at OAC in Baltimore, and we decided as a family to move to a small area called Pagasa, just outside of Manila.

When I landed in Manila for the first time, it was easy to see why General MacArthur famously said, "I will return!" at the end of WWII. It was (and still is) such a beautiful country. The Philippines is made up of a large number of tropical islands, densely packed into a small area of the South China Sea.

The Filipinos loved Americans. They had converted old WII jeeps into *Jeepneys* in Manila and most other major cities. These unique vehicles gave the colorful local transportation a familiar, distinctly Filipino flair. They're unmistakable throughout the country.

In general, the country's northern islands, such as Luzon (where Manila is located) are comprised of a large number of Catholics. The southern islands, such as Mindanao, are comprised of mostly Muslims. That's not all that surprising, as those islands are so close to Indonesia, a country with the largest Muslim population in the world.

The country was still under the dictatorial rule of its president, Ferdinand Marcos, and his wife, Imelda (who was well-known for her collection of over 2000 pairs of designer shoes).

The imbalance between rich and poor was striking, with most of the population living in conditions of fierce poverty. In the West Triangle area of Quezon City, a stone's throw from future president Corazon Aquino's home, you'd find abandoned lots and deserted buildings that were the unofficial homes of hundreds of *squatters*. There were hundreds of these areas around the city, where the residents would "pirate" water and electricity from anywhere.

I specialized in street ministry, but compared to the US, Manila was a whole other story. After all, you were looking at over 10 million people in that area during the mid-80s and many of them were in poverty. I couldn't get my head around the staggering number of *squatters*, which were people who had simply set up their houses and their communities on some kind of government land.

Once a squatter had been set up for more than 24 hours, you couldn't move them without going through the legal system. There were huge areas where thousands and thousands of people had "squatter's rights." (This could possibly even be happening in the USA now.)

Still, I think the most surprising thing to experience was the irrepressible spirit of the people we met. Their entrepreneurial drive was strong. People would create imaginative ways to earn money to survive.

"Can I get you a glass of water?"

As usual, our programs in the Philippines involved setting up in public places with a sketch-board. This is what we did; it's what I've done all my life. As I was conducting programs one day in 1985, a guy came up and said, "Hey, can I get you a glass of water?"

This happened while I was preaching, and the neighborhood kids were gathering around to watch me painting on the sketch board. Afterwards, he came up and thanked me for being there and sharing the good news. His words were both affirming and encouraging.

As we talked that afternoon, I discovered that Noe (whose name sounds like "Noah") lived with his wife and his mother-in-law in the neighborhood. We became buddies, connecting and exchanging our names and numbers. We've been close friends ever since. For years now, we have gone all over the Philippines together, training and helping people.

Noe is still a partner who we support financially through our organization. He continues his ministry there in the Philippines as one of our PALS (Partner and Leader Servant) through HIM.

The last time I was in the Philippines about a year ago, I stayed with Noe and his family. Although they no longer live in their old neighborhood because they were able to build a home outside the city, they still go to the squatter areas to help. Noe's a brilliant and wonderful guy, who's involved in many livelihood projects that help people have a trade and earn an income.

One project, for example, helped several pastors by restoring some of Manila's old cars and converting them into taxis. These taxis would provide their owners with an income for their families. Another project with Noe involves purchasing heifers (cows,) and distributing them to poor pastors in villages. These pastors can make extra income from the milk and the heifer. Noe has also helped farmers invest in another area of the Philippines by planting mango trees that they can harvest, and take the mangos to the market to sell.

As you can see, these are all very creative ways to provide an income for the families in need. We invest in these and many other projects around the world, so we can "help them help themselves" so they aren't dependent on our support.

Every Filipino knows this joke

The Philippines is an island country in Southeast Asia that consists of no less than 7,100 small islands.

There is a joke in the Philippines that says:
"In the Philippines, at low tide, there are 7,000 islands. At high tide, there are only 6,000."

Mindanao is the largest island in the south, and the two major cities of General Santos City and Davao City are located on it. It is mostly known for being "the Muslim headquarters" for all the rebels who have been against the government.

In fact, a notorious event happened there in 2001 involving the rebels kidnapping and holding 20 people as hostages, including a missionary couple from my home state of Kansas.

Gracia and Martin Burnham, along with the rest of those kidnapped, were taken to Mindanao, where the rebels held them for ransom. Although most of the others were killed, the Burnhams were held captive for a year. For much of that time, they were held in a very remote and mountainous area of the island of Mindanao, where I've been many times.

In a shootout during the rescue attempt made by the Philippine army, Martin was shot and killed. Gracia was rescued, and returned to Kansas with her three children. Gracia has continued to faithfully carry on the ministry as his widow.

This village of Pait, Mindanao, is very dear to my heart. I have visited, ministered and worked there numerous times over the years. There is a mountain right outside the village called *Prayer Mountain*, where many go to pray and seek the Lord. As I stood on the top of the mountain and looked over the vast mountain range covered in trees, I felt the gravity of the circumstances and the environment that Martin and Gracia endured.

My point is, the south was generally the Muslim area, and the north was mostly Roman-Catholic. The northern island of Luzon island is where the capital city of Manila lies.

I travelled throughout the Philippine islands, conducting week-long seminars and training over 1,200 Filipino leaders. Many of those leaders are actually still using the methods and communication skills we taught them, even today.

While I was travelling throughout the islands, Barb and our four children were based in Pagasa, just outside of Quezon City. I would come and go, heading out to do my neighborhood meetings, village seminars, trainings, and circulating among the different churches.

During that time, we were very grateful that our kids were able to attend the well-known international school Faith Academy.

To the naïve, wester eyes, the poverty seen there was shocking, to say the least. The area was much like India, actually, with its *squatter* street people and rural villages. The thing that thrilled me through it all was seeing the creativity and drive in these people to survive. The entrepreneurship in both India and the Philippines was inspiring.

Going the extra mile

People would do almost anything to survive, even picking up and sorting out trash. For the equivalent of about 50 cents in Filipino pesos, someone would wash your car on the street, with just buckets and bare feet. You'd pull up on the curb and, while they washed your car, you'd become buddies with them and develop relationships.

Lorenzo was a young street kid I'd gotten to be really good friends with. I loved this guy. When I met him, he was probably 15 years old, and he'd never gone to school. Lorenzo, like so many others, had to work every day to survive. He lived in a squatter area, and would come out to the curb and wait for cars to wash... and boy, was he a master car washer!

Whenever I wanted my car washed, I would go to him. He'd climb up on top of our *Tamaraw* vehicle, and he'd wash the hood and everything, barefoot and pants rolled-up. Lorenzo would work like a dog. I mean, he was absolutely devoted and full of integrity. Even at his young age, he inspired me.

Going the extra mile with a little bucket, he'd have to go back and forth to some public water faucet up the street to fill the bucket, then soap, and then rinse. I would always try to pay him well for his efforts.

As we got to know each other, I started sharing my faith and giving him literature, books and Bibles in Tagalog, his native language. Long story short, Lorenzo became a believer and opened his heart to the Lord. That is my trophy of life. That is all I live for.

After we'd moved back to the States, I was able to return to the Philippines in the mid-90s to visit. One day, I went to the curb in the same area that Lorenzo had been working for 10 or 20 years. Since that was the only trade he'd ever known, I figured I'd find him there.

I was heartbroken to find out that Lorenzo had died. Honestly, he probably hadn't make it to 30 years of age, because of the disease and poverty there. Thankfully though, I *know* Lorenzo will be waiting for me in Heaven. It's been guys like him who've meant the world to me, and push me to continue to spread God's Word. You never know whose life you'll change.

On the complete other end of the spectrum, I've also met a lot of hotshots, preached in some fancy churches, and spoken in numerous seminaries and colleges. As a guest speaker at these events, I was always somehow considered a VIP of sorts.

I would trade that for the streets any day though. The *one thing* I have always loved, more than anything else, was being "on the streets" and meeting people like Lorenzo. *They* were the ones I lived for!

People Power, and getting out of Manila

My family and I returned to the USA quite abruptly in 1986, during the historic *People Power Movement* in the Philippines. The dictatorial president Marcos was overthrown after 20 years in power, and then mysteriously disappeared. It suddenly became much more dangerous to stay in the volatile city, with the entire nation in chaos.

Barb took the three girls back to the States, and Jeremy and I stayed in Manila for another month to wrap things up. There were helicopters swarming the skies and tanks rumbling through the streets…and *no one* seemed to know who was actually in charge!

In my typical fashion, I felt very loyal to the locals, and wanted to stand by them. Jeremy and I joined them in the streets, where nearly a million others were on the EDSA highway. Many of those out in the streets, standing up against the soldiers, were from the Catholic church. At that time, nobody knew where Marcos was.

Within days, the entire capital of Manilla, including *Malacañang Palace* which was the presidential residence where Marcos had lived, was overrun. The government and the public soon realized that Marcos had fled the country. I stayed to clean up a lot of business, our personal possessions, legal things, and especially the relational ties that had become like family.

Our Filipina PALS are small women with HUGE hearts!

When my son and I finally flew out of the Philippines and landed in Los Angeles at LAX, I'll never forget how I was nearly stunned and speechless, walking through the airport and seeing all these "huge, blonde women."

The American women were probably a foot taller than the Filipina women and suddenly, I thought, "Oh my God, these American ladies are like *Amazon women!*"

I suppose, after 2 years overseas, we'd gotten used to the "little Filipina women." That was the first time I'd noticed any kind of reverse culture shock; something I'd never even thought about while I was in the Philippines.

Surrounded by family ties

After Barb and I returned to America, we questioned whether to settle in Kansas again or go back to Baltimore. Since I'd gotten more involved in my third-world priorities, Barb looked at me and said, "If you're going to keep going overseas a lot, I want to move back to Kansas City with the kids."

After everything including school in Florida and mission work in Baltimore, Mexico, India and the Philippines, we had been away from KC for 17 years. Barb said, "I want the kids to be around my family. If you're going to be gone half the year, I want the kids to know your dad, your brother, my sisters, and my parents. They'll have a family, and maybe some continuity as well." They were also approaching their teenage years.

Barb was right. By the time we'd gotten the kids in school, it was February. We'd been counseled that it would be too traumatic for the kids if we put them in school here, and then took them back to Baltimore or the Philippines a couple of months later.

We decided that if we were going stay in Kansas for the school year, we should just stay there for good. We ended up selling the house in Baltimore, that we'd been renting out while we were overseas, and we bought a house in Kansas.

Vanessa started at the same elementary school where I'd attended as a child (the one where I was visited by the police officer). Faith went to the same junior high that Barb had attended, and Jeremy and Summer both went to the same high school where Barb and I were high school sweethearts. We thought that was pretty special for our kids, because many of the teachers recognized our family name. Of course, that could be a good thing or a bad thing, considering the trouble I'd gotten into as an adolescent!

One of the teachers in Summer's classes actually did remember me... as "the wild guy" in high school. Thankfully, when we went to the school for events and parent-teacher conferences later on, they could see a big difference in my life now. They often acknowledged that God had changed my life. Praise the Lord!

I would sometimes go up and talk to the kids, giving them encouragement and counseling, which made a big impact. The school teachers were amazed to hear that we'd been overseas, and were doing so much missionary work now. I'm sure they *never* expected that out of me when I was in school.

Transitioning my third-world priorities

After dedicating almost 11 years as a full-time staff for *Open Air Campaigners*, I felt it was time to make a change, and bring my world priorities to the forefront of my ministry.

Ambassadors for Christ International (AFCI) is an organization similar to OAC, and in fact the two organizations are related to each other. Both organizations are originally from Australia, and there's a strong connection between the missions they support. I formally joined the organization in 1987, at the gracious request of Allan Gardner.

When I joined AFCI, which was based out of Atlanta in the US, I continued with OAC in the capacity they call an *Open Air Campaigners Associate.*

This simply meant that I didn't cut ties or even stop activities with OAC, I'd just shifted all my donations from OAC to AFCI.

Let me explain...

When you're a faith missionary, you typically need to have a non-profit entity for people to donate, so they can get a receipt. Each donation is designated for different workers, depending on how the donor directs it to be used.

Barb and I have always had to raise our own support, since the organizations don't pay a salary. This also meant no perks, pensions, insurance or overtime pay. For example, the only way we receive an income is for people to specifically suggest their donations go to "Fred and Barb Kornis Family" when they send them in. Ultimately, though, the Board of Directors has final control over all gifts, ensuring they comply with government regulations and further the non-profit's cause.

Although we were part of both organizations, we were not receiving funds from both of them.

In my typical "go get 'em style," I threw myself headlong into my globally-oriented service with AFCI. OAC was primarily focused on pure evangelism in the public, but AFCI focused on local church renewal and revival. I felt it was time for me to get back into the church systems.

New roots in the heartland

After years of living in "temporary" locations in the military, in Vietnam, Florida, Baltimore, India and the Philippines, I was at a point in my life where I was ready to say, "Let's go back to the heartland."

With the missionary organizations I was working with, I would have to go to Baltimore or Atlanta to connect with them from time to time. I felt if I could be rooted in Kansas City, the heart of America, I could travel internationally much more easily.

Now that I think of it, when I say "heartland," it was more than just a physical location for me...it was symbolic, too. Geographically, Kansas is in the very center of the United States. Plus, I felt Kansas also embodied the core of our country's values and generosity. I believed that if we could get the heart of our country going, the rest of the body would follow along. "If you have a good heart, it will impact the whole world."

With that spirit in mind, I became super-conscious of my philosophy of, "Why do some people get it 100 times, when many people have never had it once?" I couldn't escape the rationality of, "Hey, let's give the crumbs to others who need them most."

I know that it sounds horrible, but blame it on the Syrophoenician woman who'd confronted Jesus with a similar demand in Mark 7:24-30. She had the right idea, and she was desperate.

I set out to create awareness and commitment to this cause, but there was a constant challenge in getting people to listen without prejudice. Since my passionate presentation style was still alive and well, it was occasionally more than some of the *scribes and Pharisees* could handle.

Most Americans live in a bubble, and filter out any personal responsibility to help others who do not have our Christian beliefs.

A New Year's party to remember

After we'd come back from the Philippines, I was asked to speak for a big New Year's Eve event in Overland Park, Kansas. Several different churches were bringing all their kids together for an all-night New Year's Eve party.

The event was held at *Woodson Avenue Bible Church,* and all different denominations were present and welcomed. I was invited to be the keynote speaker, because I did sketch boards, talks, painted, sang and told stories that both parents and kids loved.

I was excited and inspired in this meeting with 250 kids, and pretty much went bombastic, pouring out my heart. "This is Heaven or Hell, don't be playing around, because half of these church groups are just social clubs," I called out loudly.

I remember playing a song about the crucifixion with my guitar that night. I'd hit my guitar with my fist when I made it to the part in the lyrics where they nailed Jesus to the cross. Right at that point, I'd go "bang, bang, bang" for a sound effect on the guitar, to symbolize the nailing of Jesus' hands to the cross.

After the show, I was surprised to find that I'd hit the base of my guitar so hard that I'd cracked it. Nobody knew, and it was just a little crack, but it shows how intense I was that night. (By the way, I still have the guitar and it works fine.)

As I went on with my very animated presentation, I started talking about war and how life is warfare. Naturally, I blended in some of my memories of Vietnam, pleading, "If you don't pay attention, you're dead, and you could cause the death of everybody else around you. Most are careless today. In a world of cell-phone distractions, paying attention is a lost art" (Ezekiel 33:1-9).

As these 250 kids listened, their jaws hit the floor. You could hear them saying, "Oh, my God," and some of them were scared to death (Proverbs 1:7).

As a result, nearly all the church leaders reacted by saying, "We never want to see this guy again. He's way out of the box, he's too forceful. He offended our kids."

Remember, sometimes you can never outlive your first impressions. Years and years later, even to this day, some of the people who were around in 1987 still remember that presentation... and once you've made the first impression, it's hard for anybody to change their mind about you. God have mercy!

I wanted to find a way to communicate my passion without scaring people off. It turned out that many more people were listening than I'd thought.

> "But grow in the grace and knowledge of our Lord and Savior Jesus Christ. Glory belongs to him now and forever! Amen."
>
> *2 Peter 3:18*

CHAPTER 8

THE BROKEN BONES OF AN UNBROKEN MAN; THE BIRTH OF H.I.M.

You know how they say that it can take a few months to really get into the swing of a new job? Imagine what that's like when the job involves a completely new way of thinking. The "office" could be anywhere from your home base in the heartland, on a sidewalk, in a community center, or in a tent you've quickly put up in a village in Asia, Africa, USSR, Europe, the South Pacific or India!

That's exactly the shift I was learning to adjust to, with the world focus of my new life with *Ambassadors for Christ, International.* What an honor and privilege to be influenced by Ian North, Allen Gardner, Al Whitttinghill, and so many other great men of God at that time.

Travelling, speaking, and teaching in so many churches and countries around the world can be fun, exciting, rewarding, dangerous and demanding. Oftentimes it can be all of those things at once, moving so fast it makes your head spin! Spiritual warfare!

"Hey, can I get your attention for a minute?"

At the same time that I was doing mission work and street presentations everwhere we went, I was always trying to raise funds and resources we needed to serve the Lord and His people in countries around the world. This could be half a million dollars or more, and it was serious business. However, I'm not a fundraiser. I'm a street preacher… and a radical one at that.

Send me to the raw streets or the jungle and I feel right at home, but sit me down with some "high-class snobs" who live in the suburbs and I just want to scream. I just want to get them to listen, even for only a few seconds. I know how many people are clueless about how just a little money (our "crumbs") can make such a big difference in the lives of unreached people. I want everyone to know and be a part of it.

After we'd moved back to my home town in Kansas, it wasn't long before I'd reconnected with friends, community leaders and a few godly, gifted businessmen who wanted to support the work we do around the world. Those connections, along with our connections and commitments from our time in Baltimore and Florida, kept us moving in the ministry.

I'd always stayed in contact and talked with guys like George Gool, the construction guy who'd put me to work in Florida, and my dear friend Bob Blair, who owns an envelope business.

I also thank God for the day I met Ray Murray, who was

a big business man in my eyes. He was an entrepreneur and multi-millionaire, who'd somehow gotten involved with me when I'd lived in Tampa. I was so naïve that I had no idea of his financial status or that he was one of the most well-known philanthropists in Florida. I just knew he was like an adopted father to me. We connected deeply around the Bible. We had many early mornings together at a men's class where he poured his heart and life into me.

Although Ray has gone to be with the Lord, I still feel his influence almost every day. I was such a loose cannon back in those days that Ray probably felt I could use some of his gentle and deep counsel. He would also occasionally send special gifts to Barb, so she was able to buy whatever she needed and live a "normal life."

When we returned from the Philippines, Ray gave us $10,000 to help with the down payment on a house. It eventually started to sink in, that what seemed like a lot of money to us, was actually not that much for people like Ray. They could do so much good for others through their philanthropy. Ray was definitely sent from God to keep us and our ministry healthy at that time.

Another businessman named Rick Mortensen, and his wife Pam, have also been used mightily by God. Rick owned an engineering company in Tampa, and very graciously provided us with three vehicles over the years. The first time he gifted us with one, he just said, "Come and get it. My company buys trucks, and I want to buy you a car to keep you moving out safely for the ministry."

I was stunned. Completely stunned!

Each time we shipped school buses loaded with supplies for Nicaragua, Rick would service them (with Manny's help).

Rick unexpectedly went to be with the Lord last year, and I've thought of him nearly every day since. Every mile I drive, I'm reminded that he is still part of our ministry.

Byron Whetstone has been another entrepreneur who owns several businesses right here in KC, and he has joined me in a timely partnership.

Even today, he contributes so much more than simply writing a check to us once in a while. His practical generosity provides us with office space and administrative help. Byron is presently on our Board of Directors of HIM, and he is leading us into the future with new structure and strategy.

Along the way, Joe and Carla Kormanik became dear friends through the ministry. They have eagerly volunteered for trips to India and Nicaragua and been an active part of our lives. They own a construction business in central Kansas, and have always used their business to help the Kingdom of God and the outreach of HIM.

I remember the time when an insurance agent named Frank Knipe literally handed me several hundred dollars in cash, just to help our family when we were in Baltimore. When our family struggled, he always seemed to come through and help us in some way.

I should also tell you about Tony Reyes, another key man in my life and ministry. When I met Tony, he also lived in Kansas City, and worked as the manager of a steel company. He was pretty much a "wounded victim of the institutional church." He and I became real buddies because, while we were in the church, we both felt a little rejected.

Nevertheless, we loved one another, and we loved the Lord. As we became very deep and close friends, Tony became my mentor in everything from bank accounts and business operations to how to save money, and how to take care of my family. He poured out his whole life to me, and gave me a lot of practical skills and ideas for living and growing.

Living as we often did with no health insurance, so many health providers would not charge us for coverage, as their way of partnering with the Lord's business.

These individuals, along with many other business people, advisors, and friends, have truly stood by us through it all. There's always been this balance between my crazy vision, my radical commitment, and some reasonable businessmen in Tampa, Baltimore, Kansas City and other places, who've been willing to "put their money where their mouth is." Over the years, they have given thousands of dollars to keep the ministry going (Luke 12:48).

Let me be very clear here. Although their financial contributions have been incredible, it's been their commitment, dedication and belief in this ministry that has meant the world to me.

I believe that's another part of God's kaleidoscope, because it takes a bunch of people together to make the world work. Sometimes we've been a channel to coordinate efforts and to let everyone do what they do best to help (Acts 20:35).

Checkpoints and reflections

With our ministry reaching even further around the world through AFCI, it was easy for me to get into the groove at my hectic pace for more than a decade. However, some major events stand out as *checkpoints* in my mind, that forced Barb and I to stop, step back, reflect and take a practical look at what we were doing.

Events like these helped us to see the greater effects our ministry was having on the souls we touched… and on ourselves.

My mom's death was bittersweet

In mid-1989, we got word that cancer was eating my mother up from the inside out, and the doctors said she had just months to live.

My two brothers and I scrambled to be with her in Clear Lake, California. Someone helped get some money together, so we could all fly out there. We joined our sister Melody (the daughter my mom had with her second husband), and all of us were able to be close to my mother at the end of her life.

Melody has a glorious heart, just like our mother. She is a precious little piece of my mother that I hold on to, still to this day.

Months later, when we received the news that Mom had died, it was somewhat of a relief. We'd spent years wrapped up in the spiritual pull of her trying to get us to come to California, and her regrets about leaving her three boys behind when she'd moved there. Combine that with feelings of guilt and hurt for living half a country apart from us, and spending years caring for a husband who was mentally handicapped and an intense alcoholic. I think she was just tired from the stress of it all. She had a home ready and waiting for her in Heaven (John 14:1-6).

Although we had only been physically together about five times over the last 20 years, I longed to be close with my mother. My mother's death was definitely a bittersweet time for me.

Later that same year, Barb's father, Ruben Mendelsohn, also joined my mother in Glory land.

Returning from Bihar in a body cast

In 1991, I returned to Bihar, a part of the world where traditional clergymen feared to tread. Bihar is a state at the northern-eastern tip of India that is populated by over 100+million people, most of whom are very poor. They have since divided it into Jharkhand, with an additional 50+ million people.

Jharkhand/Bihar is one of the least evangelized places in the world. Two percent of the population back then were Christian, with the rest either Hindu or Muslim. It is in the very heart of the 10/40 window, where hundreds of completely unreached villages and people groups still wait for crumbs!

As the Gulf War against Iraq escalated, you could say that this area wasn't a very safe place for a missionary from Kansas to be hanging around alone. I was always aware that I was involved in a spiritual war, though, so I took it very seriously.

I deliberately avoided the hot spots in the area, because I realized the Muslims weren't happy with any "white-skinned people" there. I had gone to Bihar at the invitation of a few local Christian leaders. Against a lot of advice from friends and family at home, I stayed there even after the Indian Embassy encouraged all foreigners to get out of the country, due to the allied ground offensive planned for Kuwait and Iraq. I felt that if I could risk my life in Vietnam for *Uncle Sam*, I could risk my life in India for Jesus!

Two days before the scheduled end of my missionary tour through Calcutta, Jamshedpur, Ranchi, and a number of small Bihar villages, two pastors begged me to visit their villages, too. They told me the people in the villages were eager to hear what I had to say, and urged me not to let them down. Oh, the pressure to *go* to the seriously unreached.

Heading out with three Indian pastors aboard two motorcycles, we braved a dangerously narrow and heavily-trafficked Indian road to get to the first village. I'd spoken to one group of people, and was on the way to the second village, called Kuti, when a bicycle coming the opposite way on the road cut in front of us.

The next thing I knew, I was being transported on a motorcycle, sandwiched between two men. There were no hospitals in those areas, so it would be a two-hour ride to get to one. They later told me I had smashed head-first on a giant rock, with no helmet. All the locals began to weep and cry out over my motionless and blood-soaked body, thinking I was dead! Was I?

I had huge forehead lacerations, a concussion, a skull fracture, and cuts to my hands, mouth and chin. Staff at the mission stitched up the lacerations on my head and face, but no-one knew the extent of my injuries. Thankfully neither did I! I had complete amnesia, not knowing who I was, where I was, or why! Scary. Happily, my memory slowly came back over time.

Barb barely recognized me!

Still hurting all over, I made it back to Ranchi, and headed to the Domestic Airport for a connecting flight to Delhi. In a world without cell phones, *no one in the USA knew what had happened this whole time!*. I stepped slowly, using a cane that a kind policeman had given me. I'm pretty sure my pathetic appearance helped me make it past the Muslims and authorities without further inquiry.

All alone, I made my way to Enoch Anthony's home in Delhi, where his family and dear wife Carunia nursed and prayed for me. (Ever since she was baby in south India, Carunia had been raised by Amy Carmichael, the renowned missionary who became famous for rescuing child prostitutes from the temples, and who created the iconic Dohnavur orphanage). Just in time to make my flight to Zurich, Enoch persuaded the British Airlines flight crew to let me board, despite their opinion that my medical condition could not allow me to fly.

When I finally got off the plane in Zurich, I was in a wheelchair, could not walk, and my face was so badly swollen that Barb could barely recognize me! She didn't know anything about what had happened, so I think she was in a state of shock when she laid eyes on me. I just sobbed like a baby. I thought she would not love me in such a broken mess.

I was scheduled to speak at a CEF conference in Zurich, but "my schedule changed", to say the least!

It turned out that the doctors at the Swiss hospital were nearly as shocked as Barb was, when they discovered I also had a fractured skull and three severe compression fractures to vertebrae in my back. They couldn't believe I'd traveled so far by scooter, plane, and on foot to get there, with so many serious injuries. Everyone said I should, at the least, have been paralyzed after those five days of travel.

During the two weeks of my hospitalization, Barb experienced many divine appointments. She could write her own book about these and so many more experiences during that time.

Fortunately, according to the orthopedic specialists at the clinic back in Kansas City, my spinal column wasn't damaged during the accident, even though each of the affected vertebrae had been shattered in about five pieces. I ended up spending months in a body cast, with Barb and our kids helping me mend.

I couldn't help feeling how close I'd come to leaving this world. After breaking my back, surviving a concussion, and being covered in blood in a village in India, I was thankful for the grace of God, realizing I could have come home to Kansas in a body bag instead. Physically, emotionally and spiritually, it was a pretty major event for all of us!

My special "one-finger salute" in the papers

I think you probably know me pretty well by now, so you can guess how restless I had become through the recovery period. As soon as I was able to get up and walk around, it was time for me to get out and continue my life as a rogue missionary, and love on the many people I was involved with.

An elderly Kansas farmer, who'd seen my picture in a newspaper after the accident, remembered me lying flat on my back in my body cast, with one finger pointed upwards to God. I was speaking in his church one day in Clay Center, Kansas, when he approached me with a new challenge.

Delmar had been a hardcore dirt farmer since he was eight years old, and now had roughly 2,000 acres that he and his family worked in western Kansas. He told me that one day on the tractor out in the fields, he felt God stop him and speak to him, saying, "You see all this wheat? These 2,000 acres?"

God said, "If you tithe this, if you give 10 percent of this every year to Nicaragua, I'll increase your wheat crop. You'll have more wheat then you'll know what to do with."

He came to tell me, saying, "I can build the buildings, but I have no idea how to teach, train and equip the pastors. You have to be the guy who can help me develop those programs."

Although I shared Delmar's vision, I was very aware of a serious civil war that raged between the Sandinista government and the Contras in Nicaragua until 1990. In fact, when we did end up walking into that world, I saw kids riding their bicycles with M16 machine guns strapped to their backs, and choppers in the air engaging in firefights across the skies, especially in the northern areas.

Still, I answered Delmar instantly and out loud, saying

"Oh, sure, I'll do anything. I'll go."

Immediately I thought of Tony Reyes, my senior of 20 years, who had become my mentor. We still shared a sense of rejection by the mainline church - me from the *scribes and Pharisees* of organized religion, and Tony because he felt his Hispanic background caused other church members to snub him. (At least that's how we'd perceived it.)

Our shared bond brought us together, and Tony and I were inseparable. So when I was invited to go to war-torn Nicaragua, I immediately thought of inviting Tony Reyes to join me.

"Hell no, I'm not going down there!"

As fast as I could dial the phone, I was bargaining with Tony. "Come to Nicaragua with me. You can interpret, you speak fluent Spanish. You need to go with me."

Understand, he was a full-blown business guy, who'd worked half of his life in Chicago. At the time, Tony was running the American Steel company in Kansas City, Missouri. He was a powerful man…and boy, did he love to play golf!

Tony basically responded with, "Hell no, I'm not going down there! Besides, I don't have a passport. There's no way I could do it." After all, the country had just gotten out of war, and Tony didn't want to go anywhere out of his comfort zone. He loved his family, he liked his middle-class suburban life, and he didn't want to *rock the boat.*

Tony's wife, Maria, was a devout, spiritual woman, and she knew that I'd basically challenged him to go with me. She was saying, "Yeah, he needs to go. This would be good for him, so we're going to pray that God will change his heart." She was convinced that he would go, and as an avid prayer warrior, she began praying fervently for this.

I'll never forget when I went to visit Tony at work to discuss this trip. I had one Cordoba (a Nicaraguan coin) on me, and I flipped the coin to Tony at his desk and said, "At least pray about going." He took the coin, we talked a little more small talk and I left, still not having an answer. Later he told me that he'd tried to ignore that conversation, but he just couldn't get it off his mind.

Still, he waited until a week before the trip was scheduled to leave before sending in his passport for renewal. I'm pretty sure he figured that he wouldn't get it back in time, so he could say, "Yeah, I didn't get my passport from the embassy for Nicaragua. I'm staying home."

Well, lo and behold, it came back in three days, and was approved. Maria just giggled, "Ha ha ha, now he has no way to get out of it!" We both knew he had to go with me now.

With Tony finally on board, we were off to Nicaragua. We arrived at the airport with at least 12 duffel bags filled with hundreds and hundreds of pounds of shoes, clothes, giveaway gifts and books. As we stepped into this developing, third world country, it looked worse than we'd imagined, because of the war. Since all the international people had pulled out, Tony said with a wry smile, "All the gringos have left, just because they're afraid of the danger."

Incredibly, now 25 years later, Nicaragua is one of the top destinations for both tourists and mission groups. Through the years, we have introduced numerous teams, workers, and ministries from the US to ACIBEN (but I'm getting ahead of myself... more on this in a moment).

There we stood at the airport, getting picked up by a junky, old, red Toyota truck that had about a million miles on it. It had been welded together over and over and over... and the fenders were still falling off. This was our *VIP transportation* that awaited us. A few local boys joined us, and took us up to where Delmar, the farmer from Kansas, had started helping build a church. Orlando Alegria, a native Nicaraguan, was driving, and we soon realized that he was the key spiritual elder who had the great vision of this new group of pastors.

By the time Tony and I heaved all 12 duffel bags into the back of the pickup truck, there was no room for us to sit! We both ended up lying on top of all the duffel bags, and our "VIP taxi-truck" went hobbling up the road on a three-hour journey from Managua, the capital, to Matagalpa.

Before the first hour had passed, it had started pouring

down rain on us. Tony and I felt like we were in such a surreal, different world, and the look in our eyes said, "What in the heck is this?" It was so weird.

We ended up just laughing as we're banging up this rough road, with one working headlight as the only light on the vehicle. We soon discovered that once you leave the capital, you are in the wilderness. It was empty, barren land after that.

"Now this is real mission work!"

As it poured down rain, Tony and I just laid back on the duffel bags, looked up at the sky, and laughed. There was nothing else we could do, really. We felt trapped and sort of like dogs, thrown in the back of this truck. We just grinned at each other and said, "Now this is real mission work!" (and I'm sure that stirred our macho juices just a little).

We were teetering up this road for three hours, in the dark, with the rain coming down. Tony and I were excited by the whole cross-cultural experience. It was in that moment that we thought, "You know, we should start our own organization in Kansas City, the heart of America."

I'll never forget Tony saying, "We can raise a million dollars. A million dollars out of Kansas City, to help people in these other countries." He certainly seemed to have more faith than I did. However, his comment planted the seed that would keep growing within me.

That moment ended up being the birth of Heartland International Ministries (HIM); an idea born in the back of that rickety, old red pickup truck in Nicaragua.

Fred with businessman Tony Reyes, cofounders of HIM

Long story short, we completed our two-week mission trip to Nicaragua, which involved building a church and preaching every night for a local village. We also "allowed that seed to grow", and began brainstorming the process of starting another organization, along with Delmar, the Kansas farmer.

Tony and I ended up helping to co-found that organization, named ACIBEN, and helped incorporate it as an official church group. ACIBEN now has 50 pastors and churches throughout Nicaragua. In November of 2017, ACIBEN celebrated its 25-year anniversary! Praise the Lord!

After Tony and I returned home from our first trip to Nicaragua, we were still thinking about our wild and crazy idea of doing something different and risky. As it started soaking in, we thought, "Why not?!"

We jumped into the idea by faith, and began taking care of the legalities and paperwork to incorporate HIM. From there, the growth of our own non-profit ministry happened kind of organically, in the background, over quite a few years.

At that time, I was still working under *Ambassadors for Christ*. I was also on their Board of Directors, which meant I had to go to their main office in Atlanta three or four times a year.

That was one of the big reasons it finally dawned on us to say, "Why do you have to keep going to Atlanta? Why do you have to work under this other organization? Why don't we start our own organization, right here in Kansas City?"

What started out as a two-week mission trip to Nicaragua - in the pouring rain, bouncing around in the back of a pickup truck, and driving through the tropical wilderness - has now grown into a 25-year-plus relationship for us.
Actually, nothing changed in any practical way during the next few years. I was going full-blast, rolling along as normal, and doing all the constant ministry with AFCI. One year we went to help after the Nepal earthquake disaster, and another year we helped with recovery efforts after hurricane Katrina. We also did chalk-talks around

Kansas every month, and many summer camps in Arkansas and Oklahoma. As always, my life in ministry came from all the relationships I'd developed as a people person. Even while I had all this activity going on, we were also putting HIM together.

After we'd been in Kansas for a couple of years, one big reason I was able to continue full steam ahead was because we had Vicky Rogers assisting with the administration. Vicky was our OAC secretary from Baltimore, who had moved to Kansas City to help us. With everything getting done properly and completely for my AFCI work, I was able to plan and prayerfully develop the new HIM ministry.

Wisdom and Grace for Transition

We knew we'd have to transition our friends and donors to this new organization eventually, but we wanted to make sure everything was in place and working smoothly first.

In reality, it doesn't matter how good your intentions were or if you had it perfectly planned out, because if your donors don't understand or transfer with you, you're through. With this in mind, we prayerfully prepared for the introduction of HIM.

I wanted to keep everyone happy and I didn't want to burn any bridges, because I appreciated all the friendships and organizations and what they were doing. By the time it was all said and done, I remained affiliated with AFCI and OAC while I was transitioning into our ministry, HIM.

Although the organization was technically and legally incorporated in 2002, we didn't actually switch over completely until 2004. HIM gradually started to overlap with AFCI, and one particular couple named Jack and Mary Jo Jansson became the first staff of HIM, for their ministry in Mexico.

The funny thing about this was, I was not even a member of the HIM staff yet! I was on the board of directors, and was a co-founder with Tony Reyes, but I hadn't yet joined HIM myself. Vicky hadn't joined it either. We both continued with AFCI, and gradually joined HIM. I think of the process as just being wise and careful and not jumping in blindly.

When you imagine living your whole life as a *missionary beggar*, you can get very sick of asking for money. You think people should have enough sense to be so excited about giving to help what God is doing, that you'd have to tell them to stop, that they'd give you too much! Although this has never been my experience, it actually did happen in Exodus 36:2-7, which is amazing and encouraging!

There are a lot of stingy people who don't want to give up anything, and even more who don't even know about the needs. Some donors can also be so sensitive and fragile that, if you do anything that might displease them, they'll just stop supporting you. If you say something wrong, if you don't cut your hair the right way, if you say something shocking... all of a sudden, they can just decide, "Oh, well, I'm not going to give him anything. I'm not going to donate to them anymore." We definitely live in a hyper-critical environment.

I think you can start to see how life as a faith missionary is much like walking a tightrope all the time. Some donors and churches are so touchy and picky, and when your survival and livelihood depends on them, it becomes a tricky balancing act. We must focus on pleasing God, not people (Acts 4:19; 5:29).

Who is perfect though?

I know I can be somewhat of an acquired taste – many either love or hate me. I really don't want to offend anyone, I just want to be real and radical. This has always been a tension and hard balance to keep in my life. It was also part of the reason for easing into the transition with HIM - to keep certain friends and donors happy. I didn't want to scare them away. Praise God for helping me be myself, and for giving us friends and donors who've always been so faithful to us!

God is using me

I'm happy to say that, by God's grace, most of our donors and supporters stuck with us through that transition. It was quite stunning, actually. When we did a little research afterwards, I think about 90% of all our donors switched over with us and gave to HIM. God has always surprised us with new partners.

I believe this was always the case because I have been real and vulnerable, and many people can relate to that. However, although a lot of people respect that, a deep pain still lingers about friends and loved ones who do not understand how encouraging and affirming just $20 a month can be to our work (Matthew 6:21).

Instead of living this neat, clean life where everything must be "perfect" and "goody two-shoes," I know God is still using me when I speak, or go to places that may make the pastors uncomfortable. I can speak to thousands of people, who are often on the edge of their seats and hungry for the Word.

I guess it's because I feel like with me, what you see is what you get. I'm raw and different…and it turns out that many people really like that. I'm positive that many people identify with my weaknesses, also. Maybe it's because I'm a miracle of God's grace, I'm a risk taker, or maybe they think I'm just weird! In any case, we've had many people support us, pray for us, and encourage us throughout the years. PTL!

> "We know that all things work together for the good of those who love God, those whom he has called according to his plan."
>
> *Romans 8:28*

CHAPTER 9
RABBIT TRAILS OF WISDOM: CHALLENGES OF MATURITY

As I've shared some of my life and a few pointed lessons along the way, I hope you too can make sense of the things happening around you in God's kaleidoscope.

After all, we humans are *sense-making creatures*, aren't we?

In this chapter, I'm going to share some of the recollections, realizations and little discoveries that have shaped my life, with what I call my *Rabbit Trails of Wisdom.*

For what they're worth, these five little sections contain some of the ways I've learned to make sense of the crazy world around us, including:

> *Rabbit Trail of Wisdom #1:*
> *The Trail of Tensions*
>
> *Rabbit Trail of Wisdom #2:*
> *The Trail to Home's Comfort*
>
> *Rabbit Trail of Wisdom #3:*
> *The Trail to Living Together as Individuals*

Rabbit Trail of Wisdom #4:
The Trail to Our Thriving Mission

Rabbit Trail of Wisdom #5:
The Trail of Your Life's Path

Before we start, I want to mention that some of my favorites of *life's little rabbit trails* are poetry and writing. I have one on my heart right now that I thought I'd share with you, that is called *Groaning*.

Thinking of Romans Chapter 8, and really pondering that whole chapter, you see the word *groaning* several times. It is used to describe all things working together for good.

Groaning

Groaning... when your body is wracked with pain
You wonder about all your hurts and all your strains
After so many years of such intensity
I feel blind to my scars and my frailties
Every joint, bone, muscle and mental thing
Has fought the fight like a boxer in the ring
The groanings that cannot be uttered or seen
Are so deep and real, only God knows what I mean
The years slip by like a tale that's told
We long for Heaven, where we'll never grow old
So groanings and sufferings, pain and hurts
Are normal in this fallen, and sinful Earth

I wonder... do you ever groan?

The three R's of our realization

The whole story of how we got here today is such a story of mercy and grace, with God's supernatural kaleidoscope. Through all the years, we've been touched by different people's lives from around the world. I know Barb and I have grown immeasurably, as people, parents, and servants, with the Word of God to guide us.

I see how that's been true for so many around us, as well. In different measures, some great and some subtle, I've enjoyed seeing our friends, partners, those within the HIM organization, and people we've served, while they experience a greater *Revelation* of God's plan for world.

Now I know that sounds like a religious word, but a *revelation* is like bringing something out from the shadows or some other hidden place. It's as if something is hidden, and when you pull back the curtain, you suddenly say, "Oh! Wow! You see what's behind here?"

I long for people to have a realization or *Recognition* of the truth, and think, "Now I get it!" when they discover and develop their relationship with God. That's also the feeling I long for people to get about giving to missions, when they realize it's an eternal investment.

I often think, "Man, you don't realize what you're doing! You're helping in this life and next life, forever!"

In fact, let's throw another "R" word in there, since we seem to be on a roll with *Recognition* and *Revelation*. It is such a *Relief* to discover the life of Christ that's inside of you, and the endless abundance for anyone who learns to recognize the gift of God, which is eternal life (2 Corinthians 9:16).

God's kaleidoscope at play

At this point in our journey, I was amazed to see so many of our donors still standing with us and trusting us! Yes, that knowledge is still (and probably always will be) a heavy weight for me to bear.

We know everyone plays a part - whether it's Barb, a businessman, one of our PALS, a secretary, another unreached soul who gets connected, or a stranger who happens onto our website – everyone has a part of this. That's the kaleidoscope... and all those little dots must be there and connected for His awareness and reality to spread.

So shocking, it's unbelievable...

I began sorting and sifting through boxes and boxes filled with articles, newsletters, journals, etc. from decades in ministry trying to create this book for you to read. It didn't take me long to realize that it would overload my brain, and yours, unless I could find a way to make it all add up.

So I went one year and one box at a time, from the first box starting in 1970 to the most recent for 2017, and carefully sorted through the information, writing down the details and facts for each year. I used my old Day-Timers, to see where I was, who I was with, what trip I took, the length of the trips, etc. This task took me weeks to complete.

All the information was handwritten, because I was just drawing boxes on paper and filling in each category in a different colored box, visually. I ended up with countless details covering 45 years, all on a single piece of paper. This gave me a general overview of the countries we'd visited, the people we'd reached, the miles we'd traveled, the missions we'd started... and the days, weeks, and years we'd invested into God's Great Commission (Matthew 28:19-20).

When I was finished, I showed my visual summary to Barb, and we both nearly gasped at how shocking the last 25 years have been. For example, just in the year 2000, I was in India, London, Atlanta, Tampa, California, Nicaragua twice, Washington D.C., and Africa. Remarkably, that was all in just one year!

Year after year, it was the same story. I'd be in Baltimore, Atlanta, Nicaragua (often multiple times), India, Florida, China, you name it, all in one year. This went on and on and on, over and over, for 45 years. I'm still shaking my head in disbelief! Looking at this now and thinking back, I tell myself, "Wait a minute. Nobody will believe this." It's real though; it's all documented.

I know, you might say it's humanly impossible. Even now as I review this, I am still incredibly stunned, thinking, "Wait a minute, this could not have happened." I do believe, though, when I was in the middle of it all, I was going so fast and not looking back. So I had no idea what

I was doing, in the big picture.

When I look at those facts now, I'm in such awe. I shake my head, thinking it's humanly and rationally impossible. No matter how many times I look at it, I still cannot fully comprehend those numbers - the weeks, months, and years away from home, and the tens of thousands of souls reached and renewed.

Evidence that God exists

If it was anyone else's calendar, I honestly and probably wouldn't believe it. I'd say no, that's impossible to live through, you've got to be kidding!? When I look at these "volumes and volumes," my first thought is, "Nobody could have done this... least of all me!"

Yet through all of it, I can see God at work, and this is evidence that God does exist.

Many people paint God as a pretty mean, old guy or "the big judge in Heaven," but I can see Him looking down on my life, with all these facts and data, just laughing out loud, saying, "Ha ha ha! Fooled you! Ha ha ha! See, look what I can do in and through you."

It's almost unbelievable. Then suddenly, it isn't.

+++

Rabbit Trail of Wisdom #1:
The Trail of Tensions

One of the most persistent "open wounds" I've nursed

my entire life has been the feeling of constant resistance or rejection... even from people who are on the same team!

Here's what I mean...

First of all, I've realized there are no "sides" to this situation. There are big shots who control the pulpit, radio, adn cyber-space. They control who gets influence, who gets their "10 minutes of opportunity," or who gets to talk to the multitudes. Of course, as a speaker, once you get the microphone and express yourself, it's either good or bad, but at least you get to share your heart. Jeremiah also had that burden to speak (Jer. 20:9).

The good news is, most people have always loved to hear me speak, and are usually on the edge of their seats. The bad news is, it seems like my potential popularity sometimes created a kind of jealousy, especially from leaders who were already insecure.

When that happens, sometimes it shows in ways that are so subtle, it's hard to put your finger on. For example, I'd be in a group where they could have said, "Oh, we have a guest here today who just returned from India. We'd like him to come and share five minutes of what he experienced," but instead I'm not invited to share at all. I have to wonder why they are not interested. There's a cold silence, and I just sit there thinking, "Well, they know I just got back from a far-off country, and some of the folks are longing to hear what happened."

That quiet resistance and subtle shunning hurts me more than anybody could know, because I understand the *spiritual business* as an insider. For example, I remember a big foundation that I was co-operating with more than 10 years ago, who handled a lot of big money. They would appeal to wealthy Christians to give them donations, and then they'd distribute it like a foundation does. That foundation would handle between 50-80 million dollars per year.

In the town where we were, the missionary workers who were part of this foundation's network would receive funds designated to help various mission causes. I was invited into their fancy boardroom, during one particular meeting they had for anyone involved in India. There were fewer than ten people who actually had direct, ongoing involvement in India. I had more time, experience and involvement in India than anyone else in that room.

I had brought my information and brochures about my ministry to the meeting, and I spoke to the group about the good work God was doing in India. The group applauded and congratulated me on the people we were reaching and the results we'd achieved.

When it was all said and done, I was one of the ten people in that room who had a direct involvement and heavy responsibilities in India, but I never heard from them... even though they were fishing to distribute money. HIM never received one penny, not even gas money.

I found myself wondering whether it was because I didn't have credentials from their favorite circles, I wasn't the pastor of a popular church, or I didn't have a doctorate from Harvard. I often wondered how much things like that played into their decision. I have hosted hundreds of conferences for leaders and Pastors around the world, and have always given them an encouraging love gift.

That situation left me with a broken heart. It may have been my imagination, but after that type of thing happened several times in other circumstances, I started thinking, "Wait a minute. There seems to be a pattern here."

It was like there was a systemic thing going on, and I'd had this thought in the back of my mind since high school. I wasn't an academic star in school, and I didn't join cliques (you know, where you're either a jock, a hippie, a doper, or whatever). I didn't quite fit into anybody's box, because I like to think that I was open to everything. I was definitely never a *brown-noser*, either (surprise, surprise).

I've come to realize that it's some combination of the social and political situation I'm in. That means it may not have anything to do with me, specifically. It does have everything to do with how much gets done and who gets help, unfortunately. I've learned that's what they mean when they say, "It's going to be a tough fight," because it can be a tough fight with the people who are on your side, as well as with the people who have never heard of you.

Ultimately, I know it's a worthwhile fight, so I keep fighting!

It really comes down to knowing I have so much to give, there's so much need we can help alleviate, and time is short. It is disappointing when every opportunity doesn't come through... even the subtle things, like not getting a chance to be a guest speaker with a group or congregation

For 40 years now, we've sent out our prayer letters and other communications to hundreds of people and churches, and I'm a little mystified why they don't call me and say, "Hey, would you come in and speak for us?" or "Hey, we'd like to support your work." I really wonder why.

Maybe they think, "Oh, Fred looks so busy. He'd never have the time to come and visit us," but it would be nice if they would check anyway.

When I had this conversation with an advisor one day, he asked me, "Do you specifically ask for an opportunity?" He mentioned how important it was to specifically make the request, as in, "Hey, please call me today and let's talk about a message I could give, or a talk we could set up with your people." Or, "Let's connect and put a presentation together, specifically for your group."

I realized he was hitting the nail on the head, and I'm learning to accept that it's not impolite or pushy to ask, especially when I'm convinced that what I have to offer will help or inspire someone else to become involved with God's Kingdom.

Why I joke about the "scribes and Pharisees"

When I jokingly talk about the *scribes and Pharisees*, I hope you remember they were the ones who continually attacked, criticized, and rejected Jesus. They were basically jealous and very insecure (remember that they were only happy as long as they had control of the people in the temple).

When they were out in the street where the prostitute was thrown at Jesus' feet, Jesus suddenly stopped and said, "You who are without sin, you cast the first stone." All of the sudden, Jesus turned the tables on the self-righteous "wise men" from the church.

As a young, naïve outsider in this religious system, I felt I was often seen as a threat to some of the church leaders. I thought, "Maybe they are jealous of my freedom, of my openness, or my willingness to go and love everybody." Sometimes, it also felt as if they were *condemning the messenger*, when they felt like I was encroaching on their territory (Matthew 27:18).

I'm sure you've seen how, when religious people come together, they have their rah-rah, hyped-up programs where you're expected to conform, to drop names and fit in with "the way we do things here," and all of that.

Most of what they do is because the institutions feel very secure. in their structures, buildings, programs, and culture. Basically, the service is somewhat of a formula: "We're gonna stand up, sing two songs, sit down, take an offering, have a message, have announcements, pray, and leave." Bang, bang, bang; in and out in just under an hour. Most churches have it down to a precise routine, but I call it a formula. Pick a ritual. Every group has one, and think theirs is better than all the others.

I have never gone for any of that, which often bothers the leaders, because their security (and sometimes their whole livelihood) is wrapped up in them being in control of that system. Whether it's in one little church, an entire denomination, or a whole organization, they don't like it when somebody comes in and rocks the boat.

Well, I've always been the boat-rocker, and I believe it can be a very good thing!

It's gratifying to see people appreciate the difference in my approach. Some even thank God for it! All along the way, there's always been a certain group of people saying, "You know, this guy's a breath of fresh air. He's different. Let's let him loose."

When they do, it's like they let *the tiger inside of me* out of the cage.

My slow learning curve

As far as formulas go, you know I'm pretty loosey-goosey.

I've performed somewhere between 50 and 100 weddings

for couples who want to have some kind of Christian wedding. They just want to have God somewhere in their lives, and they come to me because I'm a free spirit, and I can synchronize the Bible's teachings with their real-life situation and make it fit.

That's why I don't have specific rituals for everyone to conform to. Many couples try to go to churches where the churches say, "Here's our rule book for marriage. There's 50 *do's and don'ts*." The first *don't*, right out off the bat, says that you can't be living together. "Well dang," the couple realizes, "that won't work, because we're already living together." They immediately begin to feel rejected by the system.

I personally would rather work with the couple, so they have God and the Bible in their lives in some way, rather than reject them right out of the gate, and possibly push them away from the Lord.

It seems like many of the churches don't like that, you know? They want the control, saying, "It's our way or the highway."

Over the 40+ years I've lived with that tension in this calling, I've learned to love the people, love the system, love the church, and have passion for them. In a sense, I feel sorry for them, too. I feel sorry that they're locked in their box, but God has a big heart!

I'm happy to notice how many of the *unreachable* people I've met even feel like my approach is a breath of fresh air. Maybe they're not *unreachable* because of where they live, but because the message that *big religion* was putting out just wasn't reaching *them* in real life!

Eventually, that realization started to sink in for me. I realized that it's not a competition, and that we're all working together towards the same goal. I've learned to accept this, and even love them on their own turf. It did take a long time, however... because quite honestly, I'm a bit bull-headed, and I probably spent least half of my life fighting it. I felt angry and resentful that "the system" didn't accept me or care more for people around the world. For far too long, it seemed that they didn't love me, they didn't encourage me, and they didn't support me.

For the longest time, that "outsider" feeling drove me even further away from those churches I could have been more closely aligned with. I think it has just been the last 20 years or so that I've grown up enough, and gotten beaten up enough, to realize, "You know, they're not going to be like me, but it's all good. As long as we're working towards our common goal, it's all good." It's called *Body-Life*. We all need each other (1 Corinthians 12:12-20).

Tension transformed

My whole life has been kind of confrontational and aggressive, and I don't apologize for it. I tie it in with the very nature of God himself.

I'm sure the God who's real, the God of the universe, is

not bashful. He's assertive, and even aggressive at times.

That's why, every day, people have a conscience, they see creation, beauty, wonder, and they feel all kinds of emotions. This is God's way of saying, "Hello, hello, hey, I'm here. I'm here, hello, can you see this?" All these impressions and feelings are universal; they are the same no matter where you live or what language you speak (Psalm 19).

When you think of it, why does your heart beat? It's a miracle. Why does your mind think? It's a miracle.

So how do miracles happen? I always start at Genesis, Chapter 1, where it says, "God said" over and over. He spoke 28 times in the first chapter of the Bible. If we're truly made in the image of God, then we too are communicators.

God communicates, that's His nature. That's my nature, too. I can't tell you how many times I've gone out on the streets, walked up to a bus stop, and held up my little rope or flash cards and said, "Hey, let me show you something special before the bus comes."

Most people would die a thousand deaths before they would speak to other people like that. Not me, though. I've done that in Manila, Bombay, Pakistan, Nicaragua, Mexico, Canada, and all over the US.

I would do it all over the world because I was fearless, and communicating comes naturally to me. It's also an act of obedience to God's desire (Acts 1:8).

I consider probably 90% of my life fell into place because there was resistance with many church leaders, so God just opened the windows of Heaven to me in other ways. He opened the doors for me to be a public proclaimer. I didn't need to be inside the church.

I can share in the public – at any bus stop, marketplace, village, beach, etc. - and that's why God said, "No, no, no, Kornis, I don't need you to be a pastor behind a big pulpit. I need you to be out in the public, because most people never open their mouth to speak out in public. And most people will *never* come to a church (Romans 10:9-17).

Consider this - most people never open their mouth in the church either. They just sit, listen and leave. "Sit and soak," I call it.

We live in a culture where we've had more Judeo-Christian influence than any culture in world history. We've also had more affluence than any culture in world history, too.

Our middle class is richer than the kings and presidents of many countries (Luke 12:47-48). What I'm saying here is that our responsibility for sharing with others is where I go back to the Syrophoenician woman who said to Jesus, "Even the dogs get the crumbs."

The dangerous thing is that this gets all emotional and

psychological, and you kind of get deep here because humankind, especially in the western developed world, is not happy. They are actually kind of sad. We have a spirit around this culture that's kind of angry, down, and depressed. There's more suicide now than ever before.

Let's go back to that person sitting in church, just listening and soaking, for a minute. In the Holy Land, there's a thing called the Dead Sea. The Dead Sea has water flowing in, but never flowing out. Many people have become like the Dead Sea. But remember, in order to have life, you must do more than just take in. You have to give out, too.

"Impressions without expressions lead to depression"
- George Verwer

The meaning of this quote above is simple. I believe a lot of people are miserable because they've had so many impressions, but they have never expressed anything from the knowledge they've gained. They become depressed, because there's the law of gravity pulling all that heavy weight of knowledge down.

In other words, if you've been enlightened, blessed, gifted, fortunate and capable, but you don't share those gifts in some way, you're like the Dead Sea... and dare I say, selfish!

Back to my recurring example, when I go into these churches and these organizations that have their nice Sunday clubs. I say, "Whoa, whoa, wait a minute. You claim to believe the Bible, but did you ever notice Jesus spent the majority of his time out in the public?"

When Jesus talked, He was out in the street, in the marketplace, or down by the water with the stinky fishermen. Jesus was out in the public, yet now we have institutionalized Christianity so much that we have it locked inside a building! Yet the whole book of Acts flows with "unstructured" meetings.

When I ask people that question about Jesus speaking most the time in public places, they tend to squirm a little. The ignorance has been built in over generations, and it's so subtle, like boiling a frog slowly. It's happened so gradually that after 50 or 100 years of this, nobody is even conscious of what's gone missing. They think it's normal.

If I come in and question, criticize or challenge what's normal, of course there are always a handful of people who love me and say, "Oh my, it's about time. How wonderful to hear this, we love it."

Many others, however, say, "Wait a minute, this is different. I don't want to change. I don't want to get out of my comfort zone."

Here's an example. When you read in the Old Testament about the Weeping Prophet in the Book of Jeremiah (and the Book of Lamentations), you see Jeremiah's discovery that, when he rocked the boat and the word got out among the leaders, nobody wanted to hear his message. This broke his heart.

Jeremiah was a martyr. He was like all 12 of the apostles (Matthew, Mark, Luke, John, etc.), who died for their faith. I also want to point out that they were not in any kind of "Sunday morning club."

Yet now we have this wishy-washy, safe kind of institutionalism, which is why the Muslims and a lot of other people don't respect Christians. We should be tough. We should be willing to get out of our comfort zones and stand for what we believe in.

+++

Rabbit Trail of Wisdom #2:
The Trail to Home's Comfort

As I've been putting my thoughts down in this book, I've realized that most of the people I've known throughout my life will barely have a clue about much of this stuff. I'm actually a pretty lonely man, so even Barb, my closest friends, and my family often haven't known much about what I've lived through.

I feel it's important for people close to me to learn from the life I've lived, and form another bond that we can enjoy together. Deep relationships with friends and family are the source of a blazing story of life worth living.

I want to bless people with this book. and give something to pass down for generations to come.

After all, Barb and I are leaving a legacy for our four children, fifteen grandchildren, and two great grandchildren... just as you may do for yours.

Money and family

One of the most interesting things to me has always been how life seems to come back to money. As people say, "Follow the money," but you know I've never had a set salary for over 40 years. You might be surprised to find out that no one has ever given me a salary!

I'm an independent, self-supported freelancer, and I'm not associated with any particular religions or denominations. I tell people I'm just like John the Baptist in the wilderness, eating honey and locusts... and occasionally a little pizza, LOL!

God has always blessed us and provided for us, though. That's what I call a miraculous miracle!

Considering everything we've been through, everything we've done, and everywhere we've lived, many would say that it doesn't make sense how we made it. I agree, saying, "We couldn't have done it without God!" Barb and I have raised a family, always had a roof over our heads and vehicles to drive (even if it was a single motorcycle for our family of three!).

Remember, I started preaching when I was barely out of high school, and went into full-time ministry as soon as I'd graduated from college. When I see young people now who want to go to Africa, Haiti, or India for missions, but they're so afraid they won't be able to earn money, I give them my example. If God calls...

He will provide.

God has always provided for me. You don't have to worry about money issues when you have Him on your side... and He's always on your side (Philippians 4:19).

The building blocks of a family tradition

Growing up, my dad, brothers, and I would join in on the "greater Kornis gatherings" for Christmas, Easter, Thanksgiving, New Year's, etc. All of my aunts and uncles were always at these big family get-togethers, and my cousins would be running around outside, shooting guns, ringing bells – pretty much making a huge ruckus. We always had a blast!

One of our first gatherings was back in 1966, when we gathered for our first "Kornis family Super-Bowl" in the back yard. Then in 1967, the NFL copied us and started their own Super Bowl, haha!

These huge family gatherings became a Kornis family tradition, and would amount to 50, 70, up to 100 people in one place. The celebrations would usually rotate between different family homes, but my two uncles - Uncle Bob, and my father's big brother, Uncle George - were a little more well-off, so we usually went to their bigger houses to hold all of us for the feast and party.

Those gatherings are still some of the greatest memories of my life. I loved having my family all together. They planted big holiday family traditions in my mind from early on. Still today, we try to get together and cause some ruckus.

Ever notice how those early impressions seem to stick around for your whole life? Here's another great memory for you...

One day, I saw my dad's older brother, my Uncle Johnny, standing up with a Bible in front of a kids' Sunday school class. I was probably five or six years old at the time, and normally wouldn't have been there to see it. You see, we lived in Kansas, and my uncle lived across the state line in Missouri, but occasionally we would go over there to visit my grandma and grandpa.

They lived right across from Hollywood Presbyterian Church on 43rd Street, and most of my aunts and uncles would all go to my grandparents' church. Of course, any time I happened to be at grandma and grandpa's house, I'd have to go to church there, too.

That's how I remember seeing Uncle Johnny, standing up in front of a group of kids with a Bible in his hand. Remember, we rarely went to church at home when I was a kid, so I didn't even know what church was all about. I didn't understand these meetings, or whatever they were.

Seeing my uncle looking like he was teaching the Bible made an impression on me that went deep, and has never left me. "Wait a minute," I thought, "a big grown man can be spiritual?" Remember, I used to think that Bible stuff was just for little girls and old ladies.

For some reason, though, when I saw my uncle handling the Bible and talking about God, I realized you can't be a wimp to do that! I considered him "a real man!"

How far do you go with family?

Take a quick look around, and you'll see Biblical principles woven into everything. When I see them, I'm like a little kid with a piece of candy, and I get so excited! If someone throws a Bible verse at me or we're talking about Jesus' teaching, it gets my juices flowing.

However, remember why Jesus was crucified. He was out of the box with the things He said. Some people like me try to take it literally, and live it wholeheartedly.

For instance, there's the timeless principle when Jesus received a serious comment from a listener who said, "Well, your brothers are outside." The Lord said, "Who is my mother? Who are my brothers? Who's my family?" (Matt.12: 46-50).

Then he said, "Whoever does the will of God, they are my family." He's telling us that family goes much farther than just the people who share your last name or DNA.

There are other times like that, such as when the Lord said, "He that leaves his father and mother for my sake, and for the sacrifice, then they inherit the Kingdom of God." This one really hits home for me, because it seems like this is a mysterious paradox in the kaleidoscope of life (Luke 14:25-35).

How could you leave your wife and your kids for anything?

Keep in mind the ministry I'm doing, and the choice for anyone to follow the Lord, is a higher calling. Try to think of it that way.

Why do people join the military go to Desert Storm? Why would they go to the ends of the Earth, just because *Uncle Sam* says, "I need you?" It's because when you're in the military, you have to go. You have to sacrifice weeks, months and years at a time, serving your country. Of course, that's time that could have been spent with your family. Not only that, some people even sacrifice their life in those situations.

That is just one example. There are many jobs and business leaders who also sacrifice a lot for their families. The question is, "Is this earthly kingdom more important than God's Kingdom?"

Sacrifice is part of ministry life... a lot of sacrifice. But I have another little ace in the hole, like I'm holding my card in a poker game.

It's called "Eternity"

Remember, the life you see around you right now is not all of it, not by a long shot. That's why I know that whatever may be going on around us, it's not the end of the story.

The Bible says, "Lay up your treasures in Heaven, not on

the Earth, because on the Earth, the moths and the dust and the thieves break in and steal. But lay your treasures up in Heaven, and you can live forever" (2 Cor. 4:17-18).

My friend, that is what my life has been all about. *Eternity.*

+++

Rabbit Trail of Wisdom #3:
The Trail to Living Together as Individuals

Another big reason I finally decided to sit down and put this book together was to answer the requests from the many people who've been asking me for years, "When are you going to write down your story?"

Part of the challenge of living day-to-day, when you get to be my age, is seeing and feeling your body react to the years and the decades of life you've lived. In my case, one of my shoulders has virtually stopped working, and I have a lot of pain in my neck and spine. This is probably a result of my extremely physical life of sports, parachuting, a lot of drug use, a lot of chalk-talks, street preaching, and a few motorcycle accidents... you name it. Now I'm facing the consequences of my "crazy lifestyle", and I'm looking at a neck surgery and possible second shoulder surgery this year.

When I finally couldn't take not having the use of my left arm and hand to count on, I went for a doctor's opinion on what was going on. After MRI's and examinations, they discovered that my shoulder joint is worn out. The only way this gets better is if they replace it.

With the use of synthetic joints and amazing technology, I'm getting ready for an operation that will hopefully make my shoulder and neck work like new again. I'll be like *the Bionic Man* by the time they get done with me! Woohoo!

Above all else, my ultimate goal has been and always will be getting to Heaven.

I still have a long road from here to there, though. After I heal from this surgery, I will need more MRI's and exams, before the doctors know the extent of my deteriorated neck and shoulder's injuries.

In short, I've been "out of the loop" now for more than four months.

It's pretty safe to say that I have a little time on my hands... at least on the one hand that's still working. I've now spent more time at home in Kansas this year, for weeks and weeks in a row, than I've done in the past 25 years, maybe more. My poor wife hardly knows what to do with me!

We believe "there is a season for everything", and we continue to adjust to this *new normal* It is actually a very big adjustment for us both, in that I've never sat still for so long, and she's never had me around the house for this long!

So this is a new chapter for us.

Last year, when Barb had her knee replaced, she spent months moving around the house with a walker while she "re-learned" how to walk with the new knee joint. Since then, we've been practicing as much give-and-take as each other needs, to keep us going. We now are "care givers" for each other.

Barb is truly a gift from God, and I get to see that more and more these days... especially the ones when I'm home all day! Sometimes she just wishes I'd go out to the coffee shop for a few hours and get out of her hair! "Don't you have a trip soon?" she'll ask. Ha Ha Ha!

I think I'm finally discovering the true meaning of a word I never had much use for in the past - *patience*! This shoulder thing has been dragging on for a really long time, and I'm not the kind of guy who likes to be handicapped, slowed down, or limited in any way., But I just have to be humble. God has slowed me down for a reason.

This is a new season for me to accept, that I can't go full blast all the time. That's why, while I've been waiting for the next round of examinations and operations to get started, I decided to finally get my act together and write this book.

"Lord, teach us to number our days" (Ps.90:12). This verse reminds us that there's no time like the present!

Are you an early bird or a night owl?

I've always been a morning person - up early, out the

door, go-go-go. Barb's much more of a night owl, which has always made life a little more interesting for the two of us.

One of our granddaughters gets up at 6AM, and has to be at her child's daycare a little after 7AM. Although she's not overly happy about it, she does it.

Barb says she'd be cranky if she had to do that every day. She always tells people, "Don't talk to me until about 10 o'clock in the morning, and then I'll be nice to you." She knows she's not a morning person.

Barb & Fred, growing in grace together (2016)

Years ago, when we were watching the grandkids for the weekend, my grandson Evan woke up about 7:30AM and came into our room. He was smiling, his little eyes were shining, and he was drooling - like he's ready to take on the world, full speed ahead.

His older sister, Becca, woke up around 9:30AM, and she walked in like a slow-motion robot. All she could say was, "Want donut. TV on." Everyone knew not to talk to her yet. She just wanted her donut, and to watch TV with her Pooh doll. She was still half asleep, and she wanted her own space.

Barb and I just started laughing. It wasn't hard to see where they'd each gotten their personalities from! It was like Becca was her and Evan was me, all over again.

It's actually the same with all of the other people you meet, especially the ones you work with or live with. When you start to see their pattern, you know how to deal with them at *their* best. Give them that chance, and let them know how to do the same for you.

It's not like you have to be a mind-reader either, just remember... *communication*!

All joking aside, this really has been a blessing for Barb and me. I get up early with the kids, and after that we tag-team for the afternoons. It works out great, with a "full-enough" day for everyone... especially the little ones!

Who needs regrets?

I was talking with Barb last week (like I said, we're spending a lot more time together these days), and I wondered how she thought this ministry thing was working out for her. You know, especially after I'd started totaling up all the weeks and months in my journals where I'd been off travelling the world. This was the first time I fully realized just how much I'd left Barb alone all these years!

Recently, our two great-grandkids got the flu, and Barb had to go and stay with them for a couple days. Lying alone in bed one night, I texted her saying I was missing her. She so aptly replied, "Just pretend I'm in India for six weeks!" It was like a bucket of ice water was dumped over my whole being. Ouch!?

It was another really humbling moment for me.

She did tell me that she's been truly blessed. In fact, she's always said that, even if it didn't feel true at the time, she wouldn't have wanted it any other life.

When people would ask, "If there is no God, and if there is no eternal life, would I have gone the other way?"

No, absolutely not. I wouldn't have changed a thing, because I looked at so many other people's lives, and they seemed so sad. It's like they didn't have any hope or meaning.

Don't get me wrong, I'm not judging here, just observing. It gives me a heavy heart to see some people who have gone through five marriages, and are still looking for something, looking for hope, looking to be complete.

"Nope," Barb says, "I wouldn't change anything."

That's one thing Barb has helped me to get better at - understanding that it is a learning process. Even when I've messed up, I get to realize, "Okay, what do I learn from this? What could I have done differently, and what do I wish I *would* have done differently that I'll try the next time?" My failures and regrets are many, so I get to think through this process often, ha ha! It's always a "where-do-we-go-from-here" kind of thing (1 John 1:8-10).

This really helps put away those regrets you might be thinking about, too. You know, regrets for doing crazy things when you were young, for trying something that didn't work out, or just because maybe you didn't know yourself quite as well then as you do now.

It's like graduating from high school, when everybody immediately starts asking, "What do you want to be when you grow up?" How could you know?

Although some people do know exactly what they want to do, most only wish they had an idea. Others don't do anything, because they feel paralyzed.

Don't let that "analysis paralysis" knock you down. Above all, do something - anything! That's how you'll learn who you are, and discover more things you're good at! After all, look how long it's taken me to try writing this book.

By the way, if you're thinking of creating a book of your own, let me give you a tip...keep a journal or two. They'll remember a whole lot more than you will, by the time you get to be my age!

Growing in grace

There's nothing like the passage of time to show you how you're progressing.

During my first year of Bible college in Florida, just after we became believers in Christ, Barb and I were getting ready to send out Christmas cards to our family and friends (including to those members of Barb's side of the family who are Jewish).

With my tendency for shock-value running at full blast, I had a stamp made that said, "No Christ, no Christmas, just Hell." I told Barb to stamp that message in red ink on the back of all the card envelopes before sending them out.

I found out later that Barb cried as she stamped all those cards, because she hated the thought of how horrible it would be to read those things. She did it anyway, because I'd told her to and she wanted to be an obedient wife.

Barb tells me I've toned down so much over the years, that I would never ever do anything like that now. She says she can see clearly how I've grown in grace over the years. Oh, thank God!

I guess I've always made an impression, but sometimes it wasn't exactly the impression I'd intended to make. I'd say I've learned so much of that grace from Barb.

It's just as funny to see how she's picked up some of my habits, too. For instance, it seems she's learned a little bit of my "jump right in" attitude, when it comes to trying something new, or doing something special for our grandkids. She doesn't have to wait for permission to go with a good idea, and she knows that now. Hallelujah!

Living our separate and together lives

Sometimes when I would come back home after being overseas for a month or more, especially when the kids were younger, it would be a little chaotic when I'd try to take back the reins too quickly on things around the house.

A frequent example was when the kids would come to me about some activity they were doing, and I'd say, "You can't do that." Barb would turn to me and say, "Fred, you should have talked to me first. They've been doing that for six weeks already."

She'd tell me, "You can't just come in like a gangbuster and change the rules, just because you've come home and you're ready to take control as 'the father' again." We've realized it wasn't only how the kids saw things, but also about the connection and communication between the two of us.

Circumstances like this certainly aren't unusual in any married couple's life. Marriage has a learning curve, and it's just a question of how long that "synchronization" takes. The difference in our case was that I'd be gone for a few days, six weeks, or even two months at a time, so our communication "synching" happened a lot slower, if at all. It's been like living a long-distance relationship, at times.

Even with something like paying the bills, now I say to Barb, "I don't know where the money goes, but I trust that you're taking care of things." When I'm gone half the year, I can't control the money. I can't be remembering to pay this month's mortgage payment on the house while I'm overseas in a remote place in India.

My mind can't be on that, and Barb's mind can't *avoid* being on that, because she knows that stuff has be taken care of.

That's why, when people have asked Barb, "Is it hard for you when Fred's overseas?" she says, "No, to be honest it isn't, because I have to do things whether he's here or not. It's much harder on him being over there alone."

She gives one example of when I was the only white guy, in a group with fifteen men in India. They were talking and laughing for hours, and whenever I'd say, "What was it? What was so funny?" they'd reply, "Oh, you're an American. You wouldn't understand."

Barb remembers how lonely that felt for me. I'd just say, "Okay," and end up sitting by myself for hours. In many countries, I have gone for days without understanding hours and hours of conversations that locals "did not think I needed to hear."

"Now to me," Barb continues, "that's much harder than me cleaning the house, changing diapers, or whatever. That would be horrific to me, just being with a group of people and feeling so alone."

She's right. Being in the middle of a room with people who are speaking a different language is a whole different kind of isolation.

But now that I've been home for so long with my shoulder and neck issues, you'd be surprised how often Barb looks at me and says, "Don't you have to go to the office?" HA!!

I'll say, "I feel bad leaving the kids with you today." She tells me that I usually end up asking so many questions about things they've already figured out together like, "What are the kids doing? Are you watching them? Are they on the TV too much? Are they on their iPads too much?"

Barb says she usually gets more stressed out worrying about me than worrying about the kids! She just takes care of their routine herself, whether I'm there or not.

So I'm learning to spend more time at the office. After all, that's been our routine for more than 45 years, ha ha! Everyone needs some kind of *space to call their own.*

+++

Rabbit Trail of Wisdom #4:
The Trail to Our Thriving Mission

I think one of the driving motivations pushing us to start *Heartland International Ministries* so many years ago, was the idea of reaching people who didn't have the opportunity for making a spiritual choice, to help them improve their lives now and forever. We found that, many times, their lack of spiritual choice happened simply because they were living in a closed, sheltered, or impoverished environment.

Compared to the multitude of choices available to people in the Western world, I think we were disgusted with a culture and a world around us that had everything, with riches and choices that were beyond gluttony. I've seen way too much of this ugly difference up close.

In contrast, we've had thousands of experiences to witness to and support the *unreached* people I've told you about (the people who live on $30 or $40 a month, which is barely one or two dollars a day). I'd say that's what triggered the start of HIM, to just try to do something to help believers with so much less.

Then you throw in the idea of that Syrophoenician woman, who really confronted Jesus about the dogs getting the crumbs. That was definitely the guiding principle behind the whole thing.

As HIM started to take off and grow, our passion for

reaching the unreached with awareness, support and hope became the key. That helped us to focus the resources of our donors, and our own efforts, to where they'd do the most good with those who appreciated it the most.

I always go back to that thought, "Why do some people get it 100 times, when many people have never had it once? It's just ridiculous." I couldn't escape the rationality of saying, "Hey, let's give crumbs to dogs instead." Water runs down to the lowest place.

I guess you could say we wanted to start up HIM to get out there and share a lot of "crumbs." I know that might sound terrible, but blame it on the Syrophoenician woman in the Bible. Such plain and simple wisdom (Mark 7:24-30).

While our reach, methods and even our abilities have grown over the years, the same priority and purity of thinking hasn't really changed since HIM's very first mission. I'm so very pleased to see our resilience and our vision staying true.

How HIM became real

Interestingly, one of my warmest personal triumphs with HIM happened when the organization went from a conceptual place in our hearts to an actual, physical place, where people could visit us and see some of our work in action.

In 2006, we bought a beautiful old church building, on what was probably a historic site. It became the world headquarters for HIM, and we still own it today. I think we ended up paying about $350,000 for it, which was a huge (and seemingly impossible) investment for us.

Of course, we still have a mortgage that we're striving to pay off, but when the opportunity to move into the chapel came up, there was an incredible response from many who wanted us to have that building. The whole experience was so gratifying, because it showed me how defining your vision is often the hardest part, but when you're clear on what you're praying for, and put the outcome in God's hands, great things can happen.

Plus, in His presence, you never know who you're talking to, do you? At the time, Ray Murray, one of our beloved donors, decided to write a check to us for $100,000, saying he wanted to create a *matching fund* to help us buy our building!

As a result, HIM was able to have its headquarters in a beautiful, quaint little church building in Kansas City. We transformed much of the space into offices, conference rooms, and meeting places. We've used it for over 10 years for our staff, as well as to support other causes in the community. For example, about three years ago, we began leasing the building to the Trail Ridge Montessori school, which now blesses so many local families.

When we purchased the chapel, it was a huge breakthrough for HIM. You might say it really put us on the map. We were no longer just working out of a P.O. box. We were a real, legitimate organization.

The chapel made a massive difference not only in how we saw ourselves, but how other people saw us, too. "Oh, they have a church," or "They have a building, they must be the real deal." That was a big triumph, because that gave us credibility, stability, and confidence – at least in this culture.

Plus, it was an easy place for people to come and find us, or to call us up at any time!

Nobody does it alone

During the first five years that HIM was active, we had people and ministries we supported, but didn't yet have the concept we now call PALS.

PALS and partnerships around the world with HIM
P-A-L-S is an acronym that played on the idea of being a buddy or friend, and the letters stand for Partner and Leader Servants.

This is now the way we refer to of all of our affiliates worldwide. Each person signs an agreement of our terms of the relationship, and they become a partner, or PAL, with HIM. We now have nearly 50 Partner and Leader Servants around the world. As we train and involve these people, their priority becomes a little more inwardly-focused, because it's based on them having integrity and being servants.

This is important because we've found, particularly in third world countries, that there's often a big problem with male chauvinism, of lording it over each other, or of jealousy. Our PALS concept is designed to destroy those behaviors. As people and organizations affiliate with us, we teach them the opposite... how to be a servant, love their wives, and help their partners. We also encourage them to work together to serve the people, and not to be jealous of the other workers or churches.

That is a massive shift that helps to take *ego* out of the equation. It's not only a big philosophical shift, but also a shift in our approach and our tactics. I call it maturity. It's like HIM started out as a child, then gradually matured over those first five years.

I'm so proud of the progress our PALS have created for themselves and all of us. After all, no one knows an operation like the front-line worker who deals with the people every day.

Everyone wins that way… especially the people who need for us to reach them.

+++

Rabbit Trail of Wisdom #5: The Trail of Your Life's Path

When I'm travelling the world on mission trips, or speaking to a community group or congregation overseas, they'll usually ask where I'm from.

Someone will inevitably come up to me when I'm in China, India, or Africa, and tell me, "Oh, I've been to America. I was in Los Angeles," or "I was in New York." Jokingly, I'd look at them with a straight face, and say, "Oh, I'm sorry, you were in one armpit on the left side," or "You were in another armpit on the right side. But if you haven't seen the heartland of America, you really haven't seen America. I come from Kansas, that's the heart!"

They usually look at me confused for a minute, so I tell them, "You know, when I look at our country, I hardly count the east coast and the west coast as America, but you get in Kansas City and it's the perfect blend of our country." Then I add, "It's our little secret, please don't tell anybody. We don't want them all coming here!"

My bright smile and fun spirit shows them I'm just teasing.

Kansas was an old riverboat town, with steamboats and riverboats that started in the Missouri River more than a century ago. It was also considered the wild west at that time, because the east up to the Missouri River was pretty much the whole United States.

Going west from the Missouri River, the old covered wagons would head out of KC on the Oregon Trail and the Santa Fe Trail. This was a big point in history, which triggered the expansion of America.

Kansas City was kind of a frontier town for a long time, but now it's the world headquarters for Sprint, Hallmark Cards, H&R Block, Cerner, and Russell Stover's Chocolates.

It's all a melting pot now, too, but it's still the town I call home, and I'm proud to live here. That's why I keep coming back to the heart of America.

What do you focus on in life?

I am constantly blown away with the way everyone walks around with their own little screen in their hand, looking down at it as they walk along the street. I wonder if all this access to "digital everything" is as important as it seems to some people or if it's just a distraction from what's important. Maybe it's a little of both.

Growing up, we didn't have a TV until I was probably eight years old, or at least that's as early as I could recall. Even when we did get one, television was still so irrelevant to me. I was always outside.

When Barb and I were first married, I was so "anti-TV" in our life that we didn't get a television for seven years. I think it was my mother-in-law, or somebody who thought I was being abusive, who bought a TV and gave it to Barb as a gift.

I think I'm so put off by the whole culture of screen time because my life was always outside and busy. I lived outside; everything was outside. Every day, from sunrise to sundown, everyone I knew basically lived outdoors. TV had very little interest or importance to any of us. (Maybe that's why I love India so much - because most of their life is outside!)

Even when I was half-high or drunk, I was just drawn outside to creation. Remember the story I told you in Chapter 2, when I ran outside in my underwear during a thunderstorm, and ran down the middle of the street while the storm was blasting buckets of rain and lightning bolts?

Being outside made me feel like I was one with nature. I was one with the rain. I was one with the snow. I was part of creation.

My life was crazy outside. We did everything, including climbing up on roofs and throwing eggs down on cars. We had a blast, and I spent a lot of that time with my best friend, Steve. We're still in touch even today, although you'd never have guessed it would turn out that way from the wildly different paths we took to get here.

Two similar guys, two different directions

Steve Meyers and I have been buddies since kindergarten. He's the guy I usually went on my crazy juvenile-delinquent sprees with, like the time we broke into a house and sprayed paint all over the walls.

Who'd have guessed that years later, long after I'd graduated from Trinity and moved to Baltimore to start my street-preaching life, Steve would become one of the most notorious bank robbers in America!?

Looking back, it's like we came up to a crossing, and Steve went one way while I went the other. It's a miracle that I got married and went into the military, whereas Steve hooked up with two other guys, and ended up being featured in a book by Ann Rule called *The End of the Dream,* and on TV's *48 Hours*. He has now signed a contract for a Hollywood production of his *Tree House* story.

Sounds fantastic, until you realize that the gang leader, the so-called *Hollywood Bandit*, was gunned down during their last robbery. They had almost pulled off the largest bank robbery in US history, making off with over $2.8 million dollars in cash.

Steve spent 18 years of his life in jail as a result of chasing the excitement and adventure of it all. I followed him and visited him through the 18 years in various Federal prisons across the country. Then I picked him up the day he was finally released, and drove him to North Carolina to start his life over.

When we were growing up in Overland Park, Kansas, just a few blocks from where I live today, the similarities between Steve and I were astounding. We were both the eldest of three brothers. We bonded in kindergarten, and stayed close through high school. Both of our parents also divorced at the same time, which made us both "weird" in the 50s.

The whole appeal of being outside for us was because we were delinquents. We were hooked on excitement and adventure... and we would always get in trouble. We'd call taxicabs and send 10 taxis to one house, then hide across the street and laugh at them, or we'd call up 10 pizza joints and do the same thing. This was before they had caller ID or cell phones, so we got away with a lot of stupid, crazy stuff like that – at least for a while, that is.

When Steve and I got older, we lived in an apartment together downtown for a while, during a period when we were getting away from our parents. We used to shoplift steaks from the grocery store, then go home and grill them on the barbecue. We even started a club on 39th Street, just for dancing. We were way out there on the edge, all the time.

When I joined the army, Steve went to Hawaii or somewhere, and we lost track of each other for a few years. You've read at the beginning of this book what happened to me, and now you know a bit about what happened to Steve.

We still stay in touch, and I talk to Steve at least every

month. We are still like teenagers…except in old bodies! We were always very close as were our brothers, who always played together. Steve has definitely been one of my lifelong soul connections. It still astounds me, though, how it seemed like we were going along the exact same line, and then we veered off in two completely different directions.

What's self-image got to do with it?

All through high school, except for the last semester when I went to stay with my mother in Santa Maria, California, I was in the same school in Shawnee Mission North, attending the same classes as the guy we now know as Dr. Phil.

Although we weren't involved in all of the same activities, I knew Phil McGraw because he was a guy who stood out.

We knew each other well enough that, if you mentioned Freddie Kornis to him today, he would definitely remember me. I was close friends with Debbie Higgins, the girl I'd known since the eighth grade who became his first wife.

Coming from a guy who felt rejected and abandoned by my family at the time, Phil was a guy who had an edge of confidence about him that I couldn't ignore. And he's so tall, the guy's like 6'6", so he just towered above people as a big man. Even then, he was quite a talker, too.

Funny thing was, seeing the future Dr. Phil in action as

219

the big, tall, assertive guy that he was, I think we both knew something about the importance of standing up for yourself and saying what you believe. So it's still kind of fun to say "I knew him when..." (and Phil can say the same thing about me, too!)

The authentic, unorthodox, international mission of Fred Kornis, Jr

> "My goal was to spread the good news where the name of Christ was not known. I didn't want to build on the foundation which others had laid. As the Scripture says, those who were never told about Him will see, and those who have never heard will understand."
>
> *Romans 15: 20-21*

CHAPTER 10
The Road Ahead

Common wisdom says, "You can't know where you're going until you know where you've been." I like to add a little to that and say, "That's how you know which rock to step on to cross the stream."

So here goes...

As I gathered the materials to create this book, I ended up with piles and piles of paper surrounding me in the basement, plus a few other rooms where I've been digging and sorting through them all. Just the idea of summarizing what's happened with HIM since it started was freaking me out... and I was the one who originally walked through it!

This whole exercise has been kind of shocking to me, because I have at least 15 years' worth of reports and newsletters that I've categorized into areas of training, programs, trips, relationships... plus my journals with all our trips each year, that I mentioned in Chapter 9.

I've looked at records and pictures detailing so many of the things we've done in, so many countries around the world. Things like putting up buildings, working with schools and orphanages, buying motorcycles and trucks and cars, and bringing together all the staff involved for training and help.

I've seen the total number of miles I've traveled (over a million), the total number of people I've visited, how many meetings I've conducted, how much literature I've distributed, who I've networked with, the organizations I've touched, etc. I have all those facts for each year. Pure, scientific facts.

It's still stunning to me, because all this reflection is blowing my mind. I'll bet most people live and die, and never have the luxury or the opportunity to reflect on their life.

Again, everything you see here is proof to you and me that God is real. When you reflect on the kaleidoscope and all the craziness of life, behind it all, there is a God. That's what I think this discovery, this realization, this affirmation is worth. Remember, I had a radical change of life and heart that was the beginning of this ministry.

I can't escape the fact that all this stuff could not have happened by accident. God's hand has been guiding this divine kaleidoscope the entire time.

That's why I'm so keen about keeping it all going; I know this is all for a purpose, and we're being guided by the grace and goodness of our Lord's wisdom. I do know, however, that this pile of papers won't go on forever... well, at least not with me.

Remember the words of Psalm 90:12, where the prayer says, "God, teach us to number our days." That's what I've been up to. I'm numbering them now, and I figure I have about five percent of those days left. You never know, I could stick around for a lot longer than that, but every one of these days is a gift.

What is it they say? "Plan as if you'll live forever, act as if you're going to die today." That's what I'm doing!

Seeing my summaries of what we've done with HIM since we started years ago, it virtually opens the flood gates of the future. Now I see how all of this was laying foundation, blazing trails. There's all the data, but now it's like passing the torch on to the next generation. They'll know what we have put in place, which ultimately boils down to *relationships.*

What is a faith missionary, anyway?

When we use a term called *faith missionaries,* it's different from a *denominational missionary,* like one with Presbyterians or Baptists, or whatever specific religious organization is organizing it. A faith missionary is not specifically affiliated with a denomination, nor with any big organization.

The big differentiation is that we're not paid salaries from anyone. There is no general fund to pay those people on the front lines, or the people helping in administration. Instead, *faith missionaries* have to go out and solicit funds from people who'll sponsor them. That is a big pill to swallow.

For example, one time when I was preaching on a street corner in New York City with my partners, about 30 or 40 people packed around when I was doing my presentation. They were all really excited, or maybe just curious, since it was so unique and different.

When I was done with the presentation, a classy-looking guy, who was all dressed up with a suit and tie, walked up to me on the side, and said, "Listen, man. I really like what you're doing. This is wonderful."

"And how much do you guys pay?"

I nodded my head and said, "Oh, thanks, thank you." Then he said, "I'd like to join and be part of your organization."

I let him talk, while I was thinking to myself, "Wow, that could be cool."

Then, within about two minutes, he dropped this little bomb, "And how much do you guys pay?"

As soon as he said that, I had to struggle to keep a straight face. I answered, "Oh, we don't pay anything. You have to pay for yourself." The guy's jaw hit the sidewalk. His eyes popped open, and he quickly said, "Nice meeting you, bye," and he walked away!

On other occasions, big business recruiters would come up to me, admiring my energy and ask me to join their company. I love to answer very seriously, "Oh, you cannot afford me! I'm priceless!"

This has been one dilemma of our organization. We've never really been able to "hire" staff and because of that, sometimes we've been desperate for help. We've basically run this thing with two or three people all these years, powering it by my frantic energy and many serious prayer partners.

I actually did hire someone once, and for that one year, it cost me $30,000. The guy took all my heart and soul, and I took him around the world. He ended up walking away with his $30,000, and I never saw him after that. If you have a few of those experiences, you know they hurt.

So we've never had the funding to "hire people" and keep them around. When people have to come to work for you by faith, that weeds a lot of them out right there. Actually, that weeds almost everyone out.

Nothing can stop you

Some people joke that there's not too many who are that crazy... but I don't call it crazy. You must believe wholeheartedly that God wants you to do this job, and that God is behind you and what you're doing. When you know it's God's will, nothing can stop you.

The funding then becomes less of a problem, because where God guides, He provides! His people will join

God's work in and through your life. People can see Jesus in your life, and want to be partners with you and Jesus!

Still, we meet other people who get that, and they say, "Wow, this is a God thing. I'm not going to miss it. I'm going to be part of it." That was the case with Vicky Rogers, who dedicated her life to the ministry, and was our secretary for years. She tells about some of her adventures with us in her book, *A Life Not my Own.*

I have to tell you; besides Barb, Vicky Rogers is the entire reason that we've been able to do what we've done. Vicky has been a silent hero for many years.

Vicky retired about a year and a half ago, and it was hard to continue without her for a while. It seems like only recently that we found someone to do what Vicky did for us, and her name's Angel Hecht. I tell people that God sent us a real angel.

Actually, Angel's been working with us in various ways for over four years now. She's become a board member, and the HIM Operations Manager. Apart from me, Angel is almost running the organization. She also has gone around the world, ministering and sharing the realities of Christ.

Like Vicky, Angel has committed her life to the ministry, and raises her own support. Please consider joining her team (praying, supporting, or giving) as she continues to take on more and more responsibilities of the organization.

Back when we started, we had two connections and two staff. Today, we have more like 50 involved, and those 50 Partners have another 450+ of their local front-line workers with them, as part of their teams. As you can see, there are hundreds of people now under the umbrella of HIM as our "PALS."

The word "employees" doesn't even get used in conversations around here. These are teams of partners, and you can't buy that kind of relationship. We don't go out to hire people, these people come and join us, which forms a whole different dynamic and a whole different relationship. It's a relationship that is real.

Is there a digital future for HIM?

A few days ago, I had a meeting with our "data friends," a kind of white board meeting to talk about Facebook, our HIM website, and our plans for 2018. In the middle of that meeting, I dropped the bomb, "By the way, I'm writing a book in the spring sometime. I'm working on it now, and I'll need a website."

They lit up and said, "We have someone who can do that!" They're excited about it, and were thinking of ways to interface it with the HIM Facebook, Twitter, and blogs. I have no idea how most of that stuff works, all the systems, with "digital this" and "electronic that" mystify me. I've been a chalkboard-and-paper guy all my life, so they're figuring out how to reach people online like I used to do with a sheet of paper. I've decided that I'm too old to fly into "cyberspace."

I can make videos with my cell phone and pst them on Facebook, though! Baby steps, haha!.

Our top priority at HIM

At the beginning, when I was on my own or working with other organizations as a freelance missionary, I was a lot like the wild evangelist, preaching on the street corner, the end of the world, and all of that.

As soon as we started the organization, naming it around the word HIM, it shifted more to a mission to know and share Him, the Living God. It's all about Him!

For the past few years, and certainly going forward from today, we're turning more to looking upward to HIM as an organization where our primary goal is to exalt God and point to Him. It's pretty well one and the same thing, but with a slightly different focus. I call it worship, so that instead of looking outward to others, we're going deeper within, and worshipping God. For that reason, I think the organization has become a little more centered on training and teaching people to worship. If we go deep, God can go wide!

Mind you, that training, thinking, and leading towards worship isn't any different now from how I started. It's all the same. I hesitate to make a big division between the two, because you can't have one without the other. It's just that, at the beginning, there was probably a little more passion in the evangelistic reaching masses of people, whereas now we're aware that it's more important that we seek God first.

Jesus did that with His disciples in Matthew 28:17-20.

For instance, the focus is as simple as being more involved with the people we serve in their worlds, especially the areas known as the 10/40 window, where we have been focusing.

The term "10/40 window," refers to the lines on a map that geographically divide up the world. There's the 10 longitude and the 40 latitude intersection, which points to a box between India and Pakistan, right across to China. That's where the poorest people in the world live. It also includes the people who have the least opportunity for information, knowledge, and education about the Lord Jesus.

The more we're involved there, and even as we go to other developing countries like Nicaragua and Mexico, we often see an issue with egos among the Christian leaders. Whether you give them a bicycle or a motor scooter, or you have a seminar, we begin to say, "Listen, our whole life's about being *servants*, not just leaders."

We're not just dishing out money

That's where the word PALS comes from, for our Partner and Leader Servants. We built that definition on purpose, to guide our people towards servitude for the betterment of their communities, families and churches. We want them to be servants, not just leaders. Another businessman named Bob Zoller helped me develop the PALS concept.

This perspective has evolved over years of time. I don't think you sit down and it clicks in one little meeting. but the more you're involved, take trips, and time goes by, you become aware. Gradually, we thought we'd need some guidelines, principles, and a philosophy that builds spirituality, humility, accountability, and creativity… not dependency.

We didn't want to just dish out money, we wanted people to grow spiritually and depend fully on God to provide for their needs. The money itself is only a tool, it is not the point. The wisdom and the teachings we share, and the spirituality that we show people. is the point. The money just helps facilitate those values. and increase their influence.

Another point in the evolution of HIM, is that I think our heart was always to give a platform and provide visibility for the *unreached* and *unknowns*. They're usually what you might call "nobodies," which I appreciate because I am a nobody. I know the feeling of being ignored and being a nobody... especially when you look around at all the hype with celebrities, whether they are in politics, Hollywood, sports, or even in the religious world.

A whole lot of nobodies

I think Jesus also could have been considered "a part of our group of nobodies" in a way. He wasn't really in *the clique*, which is why religious leaders were so jealous.

Our Partners are not just someone we write a check to, they are our close friends and even some I'd consider family. I've known many of them for decades. I've been in their homes, and lived with some of them for weeks at a time. I've also almost died with them.

The bottom line is - they need visibility and support. I pray that I could just say to the whole world, "Hey, here's Surendra from Nepal, who's trying to build a bamboo hut for a church with 50 people. He needs $500. Will you help?"

All I want to do is reach people who could respond to these different PALS and their simple needs. That's how I'd love to give them a voice. This isn't like some international *slush fund*, with tear-jerking ads that prey on all of us and our compassion, but ends up with tens of *millions* totally missing and unaccounted for. These are people we know personally and have direct contact with.

This is our heart's desire. This is what we are about. If you look at our web page, any of our literature or our magazine, we're just creating a platform for these real people and telling their stories. We want and need people here in the West to adopt them and help support them, whether it's sending $25 a month, helping to build an orphanage, or buying a bicycle.

To tell you the truth, this vision has always been one of the things I've struggled with. It breaks my heart trying to get people to respond, even when they know us. Believe it or not, very few have actually adopted any of those workers, which essentially means that it's still on our shoulders. (Please contact us if you can be involved in this way.)

It's easier to make a huge difference

Our vision from day one has been to reach key people, train them, and then create a platform to connect them with people who could help them. We want to connect those well-intentioned, needy, and capable people with others who can and will respond to their need. Although this sounds like a great vision, it has been and continues to be one of our biggest hurdles to jump.

The word hurdle reminds me of the word hurt. It hurts that there's such indifference, and that people don't say, "How can I help this guy, or how can I help with that woman?" It seems like one in a hundred ever asks how they could help. In my mind, I'm trying to understand, "Are people really that hard-hearted, are they that blind that they don't get it?" I really believe that many of us are just too busy to take time to truly ponder this and the effect it could have.

It truly is easy for anyone to make a huge difference with even a small contribution. Many people we partner with only live on two or three dollars a day. You and I can easily spend that on one coffee a day! I constantly live with the struggle of feeling hurt that there's not more interest in helping these people.

Obviously, any of us could give $1,000 to the *United Way* or *World Vision*, but that's not the same as adopting a family, staying involved them, and getting to know them personally. To me, writing a check is like hitting the "easy button"... and might I dare say, it soothes many people's conscience?

I think a lot of people truly do want to help; they want to donate, but they don't know how or where to... and they don't want it to be difficult to do so. And I think one of the biggest problems about giving to many of the huge organizations is that they are nameless faces.

They do make it instantly easy, however. "Okay, I'll give $100 to them," you might say, "and they'll figure out what to do with it." It eases the donor's conscience quickly...but, I believe it lacks accountability, and therefore increases the possibility of corruption.

A bigger emotional benefit

This gives the donor an immediate emotional benefit for the cheapest financial cost, emotional cost or commitment. It's like they're saying in the back of their mind, "Here, here's $100, don't make me think about it anymore."

The shift that I'm proposing, trying to enable, and helping to foster is a one on one, person to person, *personal* connection and relationship. When you can say, "Here, give your $25 to help Juan (...not just "some man") get new Bibles, or help Danya get a school uniform, backpack and books so she can attend school, without having to work 60+ hours a week in a coffee field at 11 years old." Knowing the recipients personally is a whole different story.

HIM is set up so the recipients receive almost all of each donation that comes in. There's not all this stuff, where half of it goes to whatever they pay their administrators. Basically, the key difference for the person donating through HIM is that they might just have to think a little bit more. They might have to get more into the mindset of personally helping, and of realizing that they are giving directly to a person or specific project…and then sticking with them!

The big benefits (for both people) are that your emotional connection, emotional investment, and emotional payoff are all deeper. It's not just a dollar investment, it's an emotional investment.

The best part is, both the emotional investment and the financial investment go a lot further when you do things this way (Matt.6:19-21)!

Our biggest challenges, from the beginning

I'd say that our biggest challenges from the beginning have probably been how to make the biggest impacts in our recipients' lives with the smallest contributions, and how to get people off their butt and actually make a connection, as well as a donation. These are things I've felt responsible for through all these years.

This is why I'm fanatic about the concept of communicating and making people understand why it's so important, why it's better than other ways to donate or to help, and how to make it easy. All of the newsletters and the pleas constantly tug at my heart, as I all but beg people to get involved and to help.

There's a Bible reference in the *Book of Acts*, where the people of Macedonia called out to the disciples, and said, "Please, come and help us." This "call to help," or *Macedonian call*, is something I say every day (Acts 16:9)!

I've been doing my own *Macedonian call* through all these years. Sometimes, I think, "Wow, are people really that dumb, or am I really that bad of a communicator?"

If you flip through our *HIM* magazine or booklet, you can see and read about these people I've been talking about. You'll notice that we're not trying to represent 10,000 people, not even 1,000. We have about 50 Partners represented, and they are real people who have real needs. They have all proven to us that they are trustworthy. We know them, and we've been with them. We've invested years in relationships with them. These are quality people that donors can support, without any hesitation. **(If you don't have the HIM magazine or booklet, please contact me using the website URL at the end of this book, and I'll send them your way!)**

Being hurt along the way

Both the magazine and booklet were produced to communicate the stories and lives of our PALS. We wanted to share about their families, their hopes and desires, and how they are making a difference where they are… ultimately hoping to make a direct connection with our readers. (A special thank you to Brian Slater for his awesome work in producing these booklets!)

Let me tell you though, it still brings us back to "our biggest hurdle", and being hurt all along the way. Out of the hundreds of people that we've mailed or handed out a newsletter, magazine, or booklet to…do you know how many people have responded on average? (Remember, this is not an impersonal, mass mailing list, but rather a list of people we know personally, we've heard or met, or who know our one of our Partners. We have personal relationships with these people.)

Our response is probably less than 25%, and although that may be typical for other organizations' bulk mailings, I think it's ridiculous for us, considering those included in our list. It makes me angry, actually.

Come on. Maybe we need to come up with a different approach, or a different way of saying things. Maybe I should try an outright request, like saying, "Listen, if everyone who receives this newsletter would send just $50 today, it would cover almost everything on our list for a whole year."

I have asked that directly several times in the past, but I really try to be nice because I don't want to insult anyone. People are very sensitive if you rebuke them.

I recently saw an online annual support drive for Wikipedia and truthfully, it tugged on my heart. Maybe we just need to come up with a way like that to get that message out in front of more people, and do it more often. The Apostle Paul wrote a lot of letters, but he didn't have a cell phone.

Sometimes even I need to read a message a few times before it sinks in. Sometimes we've had people who've known us for years, and they are super nice people, but they've never really given anything. Then lo and behold, a check or a gift comes in, and that person says, "I never realized you guys lived by faith and donations. I didn't know that's how it worked."

Other times they may say, "Hey, I was given some unexpected money," or "I just got my tax return back. I think I'm going to give some money to HIM."

I try to balance that with trusting God, never trying to push people. It's a constant balance. That's why we have so many trainings, stories, and good news that we share. (Take a look at our web-site or Facebook to see them, using the URL listed at the end of this book)

Prayer is always the secret weapon (Matthew 6:6).

My own biggest epiphany with HIM

I think my biggest personal discovery with HIM has been this...

We have always lived on the many little drips it takes to fill a bucket; the widow's mite. I'm talking, individuals giving donations of $25 a month. Thirty years of faithful giving like this ended up being about $10,000! It was just drops in the bucket, over and over and over again. Month by month, it usually provided enough to pay the bills, etc. so we could survive. Praise the Lord for every dollar (or drop) given, it adds up!

I think the revelation for me was to find out there were other people out in the world like Rick and Ray; other wealthy people who could give $25,000 just like that. They could write one big check and it was done. For me, that was shocking. All I could say was, "Oh my God, thank you!"

I realized there were people in different classes of society financially, who believed the same things we did. It's been gratifying to discover that they loved us, and they were all in with us. I'm sure for some who were very wealthy, a donation that seemed large to us (because we knew how far we could make it stretch), was actually a not that much to them (even some people reading this book right now, for example).

I admit, the way I was raised, and part of my push towards juvenile delinquency, was because I had a Robin Hood mentality. I was from the other side of the tracks where "you steal from the rich and give to the poor", and "rich people were generally bad."

Then, for God to change my heart and teach me to understand, "You know, this guy can drive a BMW and still be more humble and spiritual than I am. Who did I think I was, that I might believe I'm better than somebody because I'm poor and they're rich?"

That was a big epiphany for me.

Not compromising

I'd say one thing I'm most pleased about with the path of

HIM has been that I believe that we have not had to compromise. We have always been under tremendous pressure to be more socially adaptable, politically correct, or conform to others' ideas of how we should live.

It's exciting to know that HIM has not caved in to that pressure. We've had the same fundamental vision and haven't deviated from it. For example, we don't compromise our mission and "just provide water." We're not trying to be the *United Nations* or the *Salvation Army*. We're just trying to *keep the main thing the main thing* and stay firm in our faith and beliefs (Colossians 2:1-19).

"He must increase, and I must decrease"

John 3:30 says, "He must increase/become greater, and I must decrease/become less." This is a philosophy that we wholeheartedly believe in and live by.

Take a food pantry, for example. This service alone is not Christ-centered. Although they can be good and do help a lot of poor and needy people, many food banks are secular, addressing only the need for food. It's only when Christ is the focus, and becomes the greater driving force, that something like a food pantry can change from helping to truly changing someone's life.

Is there anything I would do differently?

When I think about what we could have done better, I often consider how we've approached staffing and recruiting help. All along, we've managed this worldwide organization of HIM with basically only three people. Three people doing everything including: administration, government regulations, follow up, correspondence, donor relationships, travelling nationally and internationally, etc.

The roots and fruits

Honestly, it's been very hard to do all of this with only three people and a few volunteers. I wish we'd had a better infrastructure and a plan for staffing, volunteers, and duties from the start.

In our literature and our presentations, we often use an image of a tree with strong roots to illustrate the parts of our organization. We call it "The roots and fruits of HIM."

The roots include things like: administration, office, accounting, correspondence, media, Board of Directors, fund raising, and donor database.

The fruits are the full, lush part of the tree. They include things like: village outreach, distributing Bibles and literature, training, church planting, orphanages and schools, resources and education, livelihood projects, and evangelizing.

With a real tree, if you don't have strong roots supporting it, the top of tree will not do well. Similarly, if HIM doesn't have a strong infrastructure or "roots" here in the States, our international Partners or "fruits" will not flourish.

As we've built HIM through the years, we've tried very

hard to always have a high-quality office operations system. For example, in an effort to provide our donors with a higher level of accountability and transparency, HIM became a member of ECFA, which is one of the largest Christian accountability watch organizations.

A real Angel helps oversee the future of HIM

It's pretty obvious that my desire and gifting lean more toward the "fruit" side, and not so much toward the "roots" side. Consequently, I feel the "roots" have always been "the thorn in my side" and one of our weaknesses. I know if I didn't have Vicky to help me all these years, we would not have made it.

Going back to that question of "What could we be doing better?" This is it; *stronger roots.*

It's inspiring to feel that yes, we've done a lot, but we

could do so much more if we had a better root system. I believe it simply boils down to having more friends and volunteers. If Angel & I had more people to help, people we could trust and count on to get the stuff done, we'd have more time to do the other stuff out there in the world. Although this sounds easy, surely, we have people willing to volunteer, it takes time and intentionality to build a quality volunteer system. It also takes money.

We have reached out to a lot of people with what we've done up to this point, so now we need to move forward and trust that God will provide who and what we need, always.

HIM's greatest needs today

If you ask me, I think the next big step that HIM needs to take today can honestly be said in three short words - replace Fred Kornis.

The trouble is, many people tell me that this can't be done or that, "Fred Kornis is irreplaceable." I appreciate the compliment, I really do. I've never been very easy to pin down or be described as anything but "unique," but I suppose that's the problem. I guess that's the two-edged sword.

Having a *succession plan* is part of the solution that I've heard for ten years or more. I've been to numerous seminars and listened to organizational experts, and they all tell me the same thing. It just hasn't worked out so far. I honestly can't get my mind around a succession plan when I'm running a hundred miles an hour, just to keep up with everything we are currently doing. Maybe if some generous soul would send me a million bucks, then I'll see if I can create a succession program, training, and funding for that, too.

When I force myself to think of the *wicked question* "What core qualities does a Fred Kornis replacement need to have to make this work?" I immediately think they'd have to be a revolutionary, first and foremost. They'd have to think out of the box and be a non-conformist. I'd want someone a little unorthodox, like me, but filled with love, joy, and peace. They'd need to have a big, generous heart. The deeper secret is holiness and real integrity, though.

In my heart, I'm looking at young people as the answer to move us into a new generation for HIM. To be brutally honest, I feel like I'm ready to check out. I'm on the last lap, but before I go, I would like to see young people get radical, like in the Bible.

A youthful outlook

We need young people to become disciples, and bring a new, youthful energy and point of view to the whole organization. We want people who are willing to get out of this affluent culture, to give their life to poor people around them. That way, they'll improve the quality of life not only for the poor, but for themselves as well.

When I look around to what young people need today more than anything, it's both a direction and something to believe in. They need something in their lives to contribute to and hope for. I wish I could get in front of more young people every week and pour into them.

It's almost like we're back to the *scribes and Pharisees*. Many of the young men and women who see anything with the word "religion" in it seem threatened or put off, and keep it at an arm's length.

The task in front of us and the HIM organization is now to find other ways to connect with young people, here and around the world. This, of course, brings me back to the idea of the internet, Facebook, and the other ways cyberspace can help us.

That's where the vital generations live today; it's their entire reality. HIM needs to shift its outreach efforts in order to reach these young people. I'm pretty sure they aren't going to shift "back in time" to our old ways of doing things.

We actually have a guy right now, Ryan, who's some kind of brilliant security tech for things in cyber security (that's my non-techy way of explaining what he does, ha!). He's volunteered to help us with anything we've needed, and soon will be on our board of directors.

Brian Slater is also a dear brother, who has traveled the world with me and been part of the HIM team. He is very gifted in designing and creating media and communication resources, and has done an amazing job with our newsletters, videos and magazines the past few years.

I feel like if I could just get some more people under the age of 40 and train them to take control of this thing, they would run with it. They'd understand our values and beliefs, and have voices to reach, connect with, and help more people than I've ever dreamed of.

Well, technically, to say it's more than I could have dreamed of is not quite right. Actually, it is *exactly* what I dream of now... and what I pray for!

It's great to see things starting to come together, they just need a little push. Hallelujah! I'm so aware and convicted about Jesus's strategy to get more help for the "harvest." P.R.A.Y.! What do we know about radical prayer and fasting?? The time has come (Matt.9:35-38).

A personal relationship

After all these years and all the places we've been, I definitely have a *lot* of data and information. The nature of doing my kind of missionary work, means I have to communicate often about what we are doing (remember we are not salaried, and have to appeal for donations). I feel like I'm doing something like Paul did in the New Testament, when he kept writing letters to Rome and to all those different towns.

It was all those letters that actually created the New Testament. Paul was reaching out to the people, informing them about what was going on in his life and in everybody else's life around him. Can you believe those letters ended up being the Word of God? They became part of the Bible.

Likewise, I have been living like that for 40 years, putting out letters two or three times a year, summarizing what I'm doing this year, what I did the last 6 months, what am I going to do next year… pouring out my life on paper. I have stacks and stacks of newsletters, newspaper articles, journals, and Day-Timers that have so much information to share with people in need of guidance, peace, and hope. I'm messy, that I know for sure… but I also know that I'm still growing in *grace* (2 Peter 3:18).

If you'd like to receive any of the following, please connect to us through our HIM webpage, www.heartforhim.org.

- A copy of our newsletter
- Information about our organization
- Books
- Watch videos of firsthand experiences in the ministry
- Read some of Fred's writings (some of them get pretty deep, and some are just for fun)

Who knows, maybe God wants *you* to be part of HIM in the future. God bless you!

Epilogue

There's nothing like good old conversation

This year at Christmas, we had such a great time with our family. Our entire "Kornis brood" came over on Christmas afternoon and joined us for a full-blown holiday dinner, complete with turkey, ham and all the trimmings. We had about 28 people together, and it was absolutely glorious.

You can actually see a snippet of this "glorious craziness" on my Facebook page. I scanned the whole room as everyone was opening gifts, and you can truly get a feel for the atmosphere in our home with 28 family members all together in one place. Hallelujah!

Get-togethers like that can really make you take another look at life, your priorities, and how fleeting it all is. It seems like one minute your kids are so little... and the next, they're grown up with children of their own.

The beginning of wisdom

One of my favorite verses is Proverbs 1:7. The first half of the scripture says, "The fear of God is the beginning of wisdom."

One of the problems, both in our culture today and all through history, is that when people don't fear God, they have no reverence for God. If we have a fear of God, however, we have a lot more reverence for everything.

I once heard a guy joking with a saying that seems to remind us of what we're up against. The saying goes, "I know that God never puts anything in front of me that I can't handle. Sometimes I just wish he didn't have so much faith in me!"

A Kornis family Christmas, from 2016

Do you know what? He DOES have that much faith in you, so do I…and so can you.

"Do not be anxious about anything, but in every situation, by prayer and petition, with thanksgiving, present your requests to God" (Philippians 4:6).

Two powerful words for healing

"If we confess our sins, he is faithful and just to forgive us our sins and cleanse us from all unrighteousness. If we say we have no sin, we deceive ourselves and the truth is not in us" (1 John 1:9-10).

Increasingly, our generation is unwilling to say, "*I'm sorry.*" That hesitation, and the instinct to justify and compare ourselves to others, is an alarming proof of how proud we really are. I think that is so sad. "God hates pride, and resists the proud, but gives grace to the humble" (James 4:6-12).

"My deep guilt and remorse is only conquered by His grace and mercy" (Lamentations 3:22-23). When I talk about my own sinful issues, some mentioned in this short book, you may realize that I have only scratched the surface. I might be worse than you'd imagined!

I've returned to police stations to admit and confess my involvement in crimes. I have gone back to women I've violated in some way, and humbly asked for their forgiveness. I have begged Barb, my kids, my family and friends to forgive me for the endless faults and failures of my life.

Rest assured, I am not being goofy or sentimental. These issues are at the very core of my life, and many others' and our relationships.

We must constantly be aware and on guard against the pride and arrogance that is in the air that we breathe.

With the new flood of AI (artificial intelligence) now taking over the world, the realities of love and forgiveness may become increasingly blurred. Despite all this, I'll keep learning more about confessing and admitting my own problems, rather than covering them up or denying them. I urge you to do the same, for your own peace.

Let me know how you are doing. I'd love to hear from you!!

> "Love never fails."
> *1 Corinthians 13*

"Since we are surrounded by so many examples of faith, we must get rid of everything that slows us down, especially sin that distracts us. We must run the race that lies ahead of us and never give up. We must focus on Jesus, the source and the goal of our faith. He saw the joy ahead of him, so he endured death on the cross and ignored the disgrace it brought him. Then he received the highest position in heaven, the one next to the throne of God. Think about Jesus, who endured opposition from sinners, so that you don't become tired and give up."

Hebrews 12:1-3

Whenever you'd like, please connect with us through our HIM webpage at www.heartforhim.org

ABOUT THE AUTHOR

 Fred Kornis, Jr has been in ministry for more than 40 years. Coming from the complexity of a broken home life, the drug scene of the 1960's, and the brutality of a tour in Vietnam, Fred was converted to a radical expression of Christianity that has continued to mature over the years.

He lives with his wife Barbara in Kansas City, USA, the city where they've based Heartland International Ministries (HIM), the evangelistic and teaching ministry Fred co-founded which now reaches around the world.

The organization's website is www.heartforhim.org

Made in the USA
Columbia, SC
12 June 2020